PARIS SP

CHARLES BAUDELAIRE

PARIS SPLEEN

Little Prose Poems

Translated from the French by
John E. Tidball

BISHOPSTON EDITIONS

Le Spleen de Paris first published in French 1869

This translation copyright © 2021 by John E. Tidball

All rights reserved

ISBN 979-8-5948-2418-8

CONTENTS

Introduction 9

To Arsène Houssaye 11

Paris Spleen :

I. The Stranger 15

II. The Old Woman's Despair 16

III. The Artist's Confiteor 17

IV. A Joker 18

V. The Double Room 19

VI. To Each His Chimera 22

VII. The Fool and the Venus 24

VIII. The Dog and the Vial 25

IX. The Bad Glazier 26

X. At One in the Morning 30

XI. The Wild Woman and the Little Mistress 32

XII. Crowds 35

XIII. Widows 37

XIV. The Old Entertainer 41

XV. Cake 44

XVI. The Clock 47

XVII. A Hemisphere in Her Hair 48

Contents

XVIII. Invitation to a Journey 49

XIX. The Poor Boy's Toy 52

XX. The Fairies' Gifts 54

XXI. Temptations, or Eros, Plutus, and Glory 57

XXII. Evening Twilight 61

XXIII. Solitude 64

XXIV. Plans 66

XXV. Lovely Dorothea 68

XXVI. The Eyes of the Poor 70

XXVII. A Heroic Death 72

XXVIII. The Counterfeit Coin 77

XXIX. The Generous Gambler 79

XXX. The Rope 83

XXXI. Vocations 87

XXXII. The Thyrsus 92

XXXIII. Get Drunk 94

XXXIV. Already! 95

XXXV. Windows 97

XXXVI. The Desire to Paint 98

XXXVII. Favours of the Moon 100

Contents

XXXVIII. Which Is the Real One? 102

XXXIX. A Thoroughbred 103

XL. The Mirror 104

XLI. The Harbour 105

XLII. Portraits of Mistresses 106

XLIII. The Gallant Marksman 112

XLIV. Soup and the Clouds 113

XLV. The Shooting-range and the Cemetery 114

XLVI. The Lost Halo 116

XLVII. Mademoiselle Bistouri 117

XLVIII. Anywhere Out of the World 122

XLIX. Let's Bash the Poor! 124

L. Good Dogs 127

Epilogue 133

Counterpart Poems in Verse :

Her Tresses 137

Invitation to a Journey 139

Evening Twilight 141

Notes 143

INTRODUCTION

Charles Baudelaire is primarily remembered for his seminal collection of poems *Les Fleurs du mal (The Flowers of Evil)*, which alone would guarantee him a place in the pantheon of the great figures of world poetry. Indeed, Baudelaire himself foresaw his future legacy in a letter of 1859 to his editor in which he wrote: "My Flowers of Evil will remain." However, in his later years Baudelaire always intended to publish another book of poems, namely the prose poems of *Paris Spleen (Le Spleen de Paris)*. He thought of the prose poem as a means of going beyond the traditional poetic forms of rhyme and metre.

The fifty pieces that make up this collection were written between 1857 and 1864. During that time about forty of them appeared in various journals. Some were published in the literary review *L'Artiste*, edited by Baudelaire's friend Arsène Houssaye, while others were published in large circulation newspapers such as *La Presse* or *Le Figaro*. The remaining ten poems were published posthumously between 1867 and 1869.

The posthumous edition of 1869 was given the title *Petits poèmes en prose {Little Prose Poems)*, but Baudelaire himself had often mentioned another title to designate his still unpublished collection. His correspondence clearly attests to his choice of the title *Le Spleen de Paris*, which is echoed in two sections of *Les Fleurs du mal*, namely *Spleen et Idéal* and *Tableaux parisiens*.

The prose poems were conceived as a counterpart to *Les Fleurs du Mal*. Baudelaire spoke of 'a poetic, musical prose without rhythm or rhyme, flexible enough to adapt to the lyrical movements of the soul, to the undulations of reverie, to the jolts of consciousness'. Exploring the twists and turns of the city, the poet captures a variety of scenes of urban life. In turn lyrical, cynical, revolted or resigned, the poems of *Le Spleen de Paris* examine the paradoxes of the modern metropolis, alongside fantasies of distant shores and lost paradises.

Baudelaire had hoped to publish up to a hundred prose

INTRODUCTION

poems. On leaving for his self-imposed exile in Brussels in April 1864, he imagined himself 'changing places' and leaving behind his many problems of life in Paris. He promised himself that he would finally complete his *Spleen de Paris*, but the reality would sadly be very different. According to his editor and friend Auguste Poulet-Malassis, the work had become painful for the poet. Baudelaire spoke of it as a 'cursed book' that had for too long remained 'half-suspended'. He resumed work in December 1864, publishing prose poems in *La Revue de Paris, La Vie parisienne* and *L'Artiste*. But editors had become wary of these texts. Pieces such as *La Corde* (*The Rope*), *Assommons les pauvres!* (*Let's Bash the Poor!*), or *Mademoiselle Bistouri*, which portray the suicide of a child, social deprivation, gratuitous violence and grotesque obsession, were indeed highly likely to offend readers' delicate sensibilities. Nevertheless, Baudelaire expressed pride in having conceived a work which complemented and extended his *Fleurs du mal*, with 'much more freedom, detail, and satire'.

Baudelaire's ambitions for *Le Spleen de Paris* were to remain unfulfilled. In March 1866 he was struck down by a massive stroke which left him unable to speak, read, or write. In July of that year Baudelaire was brought back to Paris, where he died a year later at the age of just forty-six. Two of his friends, Charles Asselineau and Théodore de Banville, took charge of the posthumous publication of his works.

Some of the prose poems have their counterpart in the verse poems of *Les Fleurs du Mal*. Three of them have been included for comparison at the end of the present volume.

— John E. Tidball, January 2021

To Arsène Houssaye

My dear friend, I am sending you a little work of which it would be unjust to say that it has neither tail nor head; since all of it, on the contrary, is at once head and tail, alternately and reciprocally. I ask you to consider what admirable benefits this arrangement offers us all, you, me, and the reader. We can pause where we wish, I in my musing, you in the manuscript, the reader in his reading; for I would not restrain the latter's restive will with the endless thread of a redundant narrative. Remove one vertebra, and the two parts of this tortuous fantasy will merge painlessly. Chop it into numerous fragments, and you will see that each can exist on its own. In the hope that some of these segments will be lively enough to please and to amuse you, I venture to dedicate to you the entire serpent.

I have a little confession to make. It was while perusing, for at least the twentieth time, the famous *Gaspard de la Nuit*, by Aloysius Bertrand (doesn't a book known to you, to me, and to some of our friends have every right to be called famous?), that the idea came to me to attempt something similar, and to apply to the description of modern life, or rather of a modern and more abstract life, the process that he had applied in the depiction of ancient life, so strangely picturesque.

Which of us has not, in his moments of ambition, dreamed of the miracle of a poetic prose, musical but without rhythm or rhyme, supple enough and striking enough to adapt to the lyrical movements of the soul, to the undulations of reverie, to the sudden jolts of consciousness?

It is from frequenting great cities, from the mingling of their innumerable connections, that this obsessive ideal is born. You yourself, my dear friend, have you not tried to translate into song the strident cry of the Glazier, and to express in lyrical prose all the distressing suggestions that cry sends up to the rooftops, through the heavy mists of the street?

But to be honest, I fear that my obsession has not brought

To Arsène Houssaye

me felicity. As soon as I had begun the work, I saw that not only did I remain far from my mysterious and brilliant model, but moreover that I was doing something (if it can be called *something*) oddly different, an accident of which anyone other than me would doubtless be proud, but which can only profoundly humiliate a mind which considers it the highest honour of the poet to achieve exactly what he has set out to do.

Devotedly yours,

C. B.

Paris Spleen

I. The Stranger

—Tell me, enigmatic man, whom do you love best? Your father, you mother, your sister, or your brother?

—I have neither father, mother, sister, nor brother.

—Your friends?

—You are using a word whose meaning eludes me to this day.

—Your country?

—I have no idea on which latitude it is situated.

—Beauty?

—I would willingly love that immortal goddess.

—Gold?

—I hate it as you hate God.

—What *do* you love then, extraordinary stranger?

—I love the clouds ... the passing clouds ... up there ... way up there ... the wonderful clouds!

II. The Old Woman's Despair

The wizened old woman was overjoyed when she saw the pretty baby that everyone was making such a fuss of, that everyone was so keen to please; such an adorable little being, as fragile as the old woman herself, and like her lacking both teeth and hair.

And she approached the child all nods and smiles.

But the terrified child recoiled from the caresses of the decrepit old crone, howling the house down.

Whereupon the old woman withdrew once more into her eternal solitude, weeping in a corner and saying to herself: "Alas, we sad old women can no longer please anyone, not even innocent little children, in whom we arouse horror when all we want is to show them love and affection!"

III. The Artist's Confiteor

How penetrating those late autumn afternoons can be! Ah! penetrating to the point of pain! For there are certain delicious sensations whose ambiguity does not exclude their intensity; and there is no sharper point than that of the Infinite.

How delightful to drown one's gaze in the immensity of the sky and the sea! Solitude, silence, incomparable chastity of the azure! A tiny sail quivering on the horizon, which by its smallness and isolation mimics my hapless existence, the monotonous melody of the waves, all these things think through me, or I think through them (for in the grandeur of reverie, the *I* is soon lost); I say they think, but musically and picturesquely, without quibble, syllogism, or deduction.

Yet these thoughts, whether they spring from me or from things, soon become too intense. Voluptuous energy creates unease and actual pain. My overstretched nerves produce only acute and painful vibrations.

And now the depth of the sky afflicts me; its limpidity exasperates me. The insensibility of the sea and the immutability of the scene repulse me. ... Ah! must one suffer eternally, or eternally flee from beauty? Nature, enchantress without pity, ever-victorious rival, let me be! Stop tempting my desires and my pride! The study of beauty is a duel in which the artist cries out in terror before being vanquished.

IV. A Joker

New Year's Day. Pandemonium. A chaos of mud and snow churned up by a thousand carriage wheels; an orgy of toys and confections; a cauldron of cupidity and despair; the authorised frenzy of a great city, designed to disturb the mind of the most resilient loner.

Amid all this clamour and brouhaha, a donkey was trotting along at a lively pace, harried by a bumpkin armed with a whip.

As the donkey was about to turn a corner, a handsome gentleman, finely gloved, cruelly cravatted and clad in pristine apparel, bowed ostentatiously before the humble beast and said, raising his hat: "I wish you a prosperous and happy new year!" Then he turned to face his scant entourage with an air of pompous self-satisfaction, no doubt expecting them to add their approval to his own gratification.

The donkey paid no heed to this elegant prankster and carried on trotting earnestly to where duty called.

For my part, I was suddenly seized by an inordinate rage against that pompous imbecile, who seemed to me to encapsulate the very essence of French wit.

V. The Double Room

A room that is like a dream, a truly spiritual room, where the stagnant atmosphere is tinted with hints of pink and blue.

Here the soul bathes in idleness, scented with regret and desire. The ambience is crepuscular, bluish, pinkish, a voluptuous reverie during an eclipse.

Each piece of low, elongated, languid furniture seems to have a somnambular, vegetal, or mineral existence. The fabrics speak a silent language, like flowers, skies, or setting suns.

No artistic abominations defile the walls. Positive, defined art is a blasphemy compared to the pure dream, the unanalysed impression. Here reigns a harmonious blend of light and darkness.

A barely perceptible fragrance of the most exquisite selection, mingled with a hint of humidity, floats in an atmosphere where hothouse sensations lull the drowsy spirit.

Snowdrifts of muslin cascade abundantly around the windows and the bed, upon which lies the Idol, the empress of dreams. But how did she come here? Who brought her? What magic power has installed her upon this throne of reverie and sensuality? No matter! She is here! I recognise her.

Those are indeed the eyes whose flame pierces the twilight; subtle, terrible eyes whose fearsome malice I know so well! They attract, subjugate, and devour the indiscreet gaze. I have often studied those black stars

The Double Room

that command both curiosity and admiration.

To what benevolent demon am I indebted for this all-pervading atmosphere of mystery, silence, peace, and fragrance? O bliss! What we like to call life, even at its most wondrously expansive, has nothing in common with this supreme life that I now know and savour minute by minute, second by second!

No! There are no more minutes, no more seconds! Time has disappeared; it is Eternity that reigns, an eternity of delights!

Suddenly I heard a loud, nightmarish knocking at the door, and I felt as if I had been dealt a pickaxe blow to my stomach.

And then a Spectre entered. A bailiff perhaps, come to torment me in the name of the law? Or some wretched trollop come to cry misery and add the trivialities of her life to the sorrows of mine? Or a publisher's runner come to demand the next instalment of a manuscript?

The heavenly room, the Idol, the empress of dreams, the *Sylphide*, as the great René would say, all that enchantment vanished with the Spectre's brutal knock.

Horror! I remember! I remember! Yes! This hovel, this abode of eternal ennui, is indeed my own: the same stupid, dusty, dilapidated furniture; the fireplace with neither flame nor ember, soiled by sputum; the forlorn windows where the rain has traced furrows in the dust; the manuscripts, erased or incomplete; the yearbook in which the pencil has marked the dreaded dates!

The Double Room

And that otherworldly aroma with which my refined sensibility had been intoxicated is supplanted by the rank odour of stale tobacco mingled with an indescribably noisome mustiness! Here we now breathe the putridity of desolation.

In this narrow world, so filled with repulsion, just one familiar object smiles at me: the vial of laudanum, that fearsome old paramour, and alas like all paramours as generous in caresses as in perfidy.

Yes indeed! Time has reappeared; Time now reigns supreme; and along with that hideous old man comes his entire fiendish retinue of Memories, Regrets, Phobias, Convulsions, Anxieties, Nightmares, and Neuroses.

You can be sure that the seconds are now strongly and solemnly accentuated, and each one, leaping from the clock, says: "I am Life, intolerable, implacable Life!"

There is but one Second in human life whose task is to announce good news, the *good news* that fills us all with inexplicable dread.

Yes! Time reigns: he has resumed his brutal tyranny. And he prods me, as if I were an ox, with his double-edged goad: "Gee up, donkey! Giddy up, slave! Live and be damned!"

VI. To Each His Chimera

Under a vast grey sky, on a great dusty plain, with no pathways, no grass, not even a thistle or a nettle, I came upon a group of men walking with a stooped posture.

Each carried on his back an enormous Chimera, as heavy as a sack of flour or coal, or the kitbag of a Roman foot soldier.

But the monstrous beast was no deadweight; on the contrary, it surrounded and oppressed the man with its flexible and powerful muscles; it gripped the chest of its mount with its two great claws; and its stupendous head rose above and over the man's brow, like one of those fearsome helmets worn by ancient warriors in the hope of augmenting the enemy's terror.

I asked one of the men where they were going. He replied that neither he nor any of the others had the slightest idea; but they were obviously going somewhere, since they were all driven by an overwhelming need to walk.

There is one curious thing worth noting: none of those travellers appeared bothered by the ferocious beast hanging from his neck and clinging to his back; it was as if each considered it to be a part of himself. None of those weary, serious faces displayed any hint of despair; beneath the splenetic dome of the sky, their feet covered in the dust of an earth as desolate as that sky, they plodded on with the resigned expression of those who are condemned to hope forever.

And the cortege passed by me and sank into the haze of the horizon, where the rounded surface of the planet

To Each His Chimera

slips away from the curiosity of the human gaze.

For a few moments I endeavoured to fathom the mystery; but soon irresistible Indifference descended upon me, and I was more heavily afflicted than they were by their crushing Chimeras.

VII. The Fool and the Venus

What a splendid day! The vast park swoons beneath the sun's ardent gaze, like youth under Love's dominion.

No sound is heard to express the universal ecstasy of things; even the waters seem to be sleeping. Quite unlike human festivities, this is an orgy of silence.

It is as if an ever-increasing light makes everything sparkle more and more; as if the excited flowers are burning with the desire to rival the azure of the sky with the energy of their colours, and as if the heat, rendering visible their fragrance, causes it to rise like smoke towards the sun.

However, in the midst of this universal joy, I caught sight of an afflicted being.

At the feet of a colossal Venus, one of those bogus fools, those voluntary buffoons employed to amuse kings beset by Remorse or Ennui, decked out in a gaudy, ridiculous costume, with horns and bells on his head, crouching against the pedestal, raises his tear-filled eyes to the immortal Goddess.

And his eyes are saying: "I am the least and most solitary of beings, denied love or friendship, and thus inferior to even the most imperfect of animals. Yet I too was created to understand and discern immortal Beauty! Ah! Goddess! Pity me in my sorrow and delusion!"

But the implacable Venus just gazes at some distant object with her eyes of marble.

VIII. The Dog and the Vial

"Here doggie, good doggie, nice doggie, come and smell this stunning fragrance, purchased from the best perfumer in town."

And the dog, wagging his tail, which is I believe a sign of good humour among these poor creatures, approaches and puts his damp, inquisitive nose to the uncorked vial; then, recoiling abruptly in dismay, he barks at me, as if in reproach.

"You wretched dog! If I had offered you a bag of excrement, you would have sniffed at it with gusto and perhaps even devoured it. Ungrateful companion of my wretched life, you are just like the public, who should never be offered delicate perfumes that exasperate them, but rather some carefully chosen swill."

IX. The Bad Glazier

There are certain purely contemplative natures that are entirely unsuited to action, which nevertheless, driven by some strange and unexplained impulse, sometimes act with a rapidity of which they would never have thought themselves capable.

One such who, fearing that his concierge might have some distressing news for him, skulks timorously for an hour outside his door without daring to enter, or who holds on to a letter for two weeks without opening it, or who only after six months resigns himself to dealing with a formality that has needed seeing to for a year, sometimes feels abruptly precipitated into action by an irresistible force, like an arrow from a bow. The moralist and the physician, who claim to know everything, are unable to explain how such insane energy can come so suddenly to these languid, voluptuous souls, and how, incapable of accomplishing the simplest and most necessary tasks, they find at a certain moment the supreme courage to perform the most absurd and often even the most dangerous acts.

One of my friends, the most inoffensive dreamer who ever lived, once set fire to a forest to see, so he said, if the fire would spread as rapidly as people generally claim. Ten times in succession, the experiment failed; but on the eleventh occasion it succeeded only too well.

Another might light a cigar next to a powder keg, just to see, to discover, to tempt fate, to force himself to demonstrate his energy, to play the gambler, to experience the thrill of anxiety, for no reason, on a whim, for want of something better to do.

The Bad Glazier

It is a kind of energy that springs from boredom and reverie, and those in whom it manifests itself so readily are, in general, as I have said, the most lethargic and introspective of beings.

Another, so timid he even lowers his eyes when men look at him, so timid he has to muster all his pathetic courage to enter a café or approach a theatre box office, where the employees seem to him to be invested with the majesty of Minos, Aeacus or Rhadamanthus, will suddenly throw his arms around some old man in the street and kiss him enthusiastically in front of the bemused bystanders.

Why? because the man's features were irresistibly appealing to him? Perhaps, but it is more plausible to suppose that he himself does not know why.

I have more than once been the victim of one of these crises and impulses, which gives us reason to believe that malicious Demons can slip inside us and make us carry out, unbeknown to us, their most absurd desires.

One morning I had risen in a joyless, sombre mood, wearied by sloth, and driven, it seemed to me, to perform some great, dazzling feat; and I opened the window, alas!

(Please note that the urge to play a practical joke is, in certain people, not the result of any plan or scheme, but of a random impulse, the strength of which contributes greatly to that desire, hysterical according to doctors, satanic according to those who think a little more deeply than doctors, which impels us irresistibly towards any number of dangerous or inappropriate actions.)

The Bad Glazier

The first person I saw in the street was a glazier whose strident, discordant cry ascended towards me through the heavy, filthy Parisian air. It would by the way be impossible for me to say why this poor man aroused in me a hatred that was as sudden as it was despotic.

"Hey!" I shouted, "you down there, come on up!" As I waited it dawned on me, not without some delight, that as the room was on the sixth floor and the stairway was very narrow, the man would have some difficulty negotiating his ascent and would knock the corners of his fragile merchandise at various points along the way.

Finally, he appeared. I examined with curiosity all his panes of glass, and I said to him: "What? you have no coloured glass? No pink, red or blue glass, no magic glass, no windows of paradise? What an impudent fellow you are! You have the nerve to walk around a poor neighbourhood, and you don't even have any glass that shows life in beauty!" And I promptly pushed him back towards the stairs, where he stumbled, muttering under his breath.

I went to the balcony and picked up a small pot of flowers, and when the man reappeared on the pavement below, I let go of my war machine which fell straight down onto the rear edge of his pack. The impact knocked him off his feet, completely shattering his meagre itinerant fortune with the ear-splitting clatter of a glass palace being struck by lightning.

And intoxicated by my act of folly, I shouted at him furiously: "Life in beauty! Life in beauty!"

The Bad Glazier

Such hare-brained pranks are not without danger, and one can often pay dearly for them. But what does an eternity of damnation matter to someone who has found in a single moment an infinity of joy?

X. At One in the Morning

At last! Alone! The only sound to be heard is the rumbling of a few tardy, ramshackle hackney cabs. For a few hours we shall have silence, if not sleep. At last! The tyranny of the human face has disappeared, and I alone will be the cause of my suffering.

At last! I may now relax in a bath of darkness! First, a double turn of the lock: It seems to me that this turn of the key will enhance my solitude and strengthen the barricades that now separate me from the world.

Horrible life! Horrible city! Let's review the day: met several men of letters, one of whom wanted to know if one can get to Russia by land (no doubt he thinks Russia is an island); argued at length with a magazine editor, who to each of my objections replied: "We are all respectable people here," which implies that all the other papers are run by scoundrels; greeted some twenty individuals, of whom fifteen were unknown to me; distributed handshakes in a similar proportion, without having taken the precaution of buying gloves; went up, to kill some time during a shower, to see a trollop who begged me to design a Venus costume for her; toadied to a theatre director who said, showing me the door: "You might do well to speak to Z… he's the dullest, most stupid and most revered of all my writers, so you might get somewhere with him. Talk to him, and then we'll see"; boasted (why?) of several odious acts that I hadn't even committed, and spinelessly denied a number of other misdeeds that I had cheerfully accomplished, culpable bravado, criminal disrespect for human decency; refused a small favour to a friend and gave a written testimonial to an absolute scoundrel! phew! are we done?

At One in the Morning

Annoyed with everyone and annoyed with myself, I would really like to make amends and recover some self-respect in the silence and solitude of the night. Souls of those I have loved, souls of those I have sung, strengthen me, sustain me, rid me of falsehood and the corrupting vapours of the world, and you, my Lord God, grant me the grace to write some beautiful verses which prove to me that I am not the least of men, that I am not inferior to those whom I scorn!

XI. The Wild Woman and the Little Mistress

"Really, my dear, you weary me without measure or mercy; it would seem, listening to your sighs, that you suffer more than the sexagenarian gleaners and the old beggar women who pick up scraps of bread outside tavern doors.

"If your sighs at least expressed remorse, they would do you some credit; but they merely convey the contentment of well-being and the languor of repose. And then there are your endless platitudes such as 'Love me well! I need that so much! Console me this way, caress me that way!' Listen, I want to find a cure for you. Two cents' worth at a local fair should suffice; we don't need to go any further afield.

"Now please take a close look at that steel cage in which, howling like one of the damned, rattling the bars like an orangutan desperate to return to its native land, imitating to perfection first a tiger's circular leaps, then a polar bear's ridiculous waddle, that hairy monster whose shape is vaguely reminiscent of your own.

"That monster is one of those animals that one generally calls 'my angel'! — that is to say, a woman. The other monster with her, the one shouting his head off and brandishing a stick, is her husband. He has shackled his lawful wife like a beast, and he displays her at suburban fairs, all with official authorisation of course.

"Watch closely! See with what voracity (unfeigned perhaps!) she tears apart live rabbits and squawking hens that her keeper throws to her. 'Come now,' he says, 'you don't have to eat it all at once,' and with those wise words he cruelly snatches away her prey, whose unwound innards remain momentarily clinging to the teeth of the ferocious beast, I mean the woman.

"Right then! A good whack of the stick to calm her down, for she's casting an awesomely covetous eye in the direction of the snatched food. Good God! That stick is no stage prop; did you hear the flesh resound, despite the fake fur? And with her eyes almost jumping out of her head, she's now howling more naturally. In her rage, she's sending out more sparks than a blacksmith's anvil.

"Such are the conjugal rites of these two descendants of Adam and Eve, these creations of your hands, O my God! This woman is clearly not happy, although the titillating delights of notoriety are perhaps not unknown to her. There exist more irreparable woes, and with no compensations. But in the world into which she has been cast it has probably never occurred to her that a woman might deserve any other fate.

"And now back to us, my precious darling! In view of the hells that inhabit this world, what do you expect me to think of your nice little hell, you who only ever recline upon fabrics as soft as your skin, who eat only cooked meats that a skilful servant has carefully cut into slices for you?

"And how should I interpret all these little sighs that swell your perfumed breast, my lusty coquette? And all these affectations learned from books, and this relentless melancholy, designed to arouse anything but pity in the observer? To be honest, I sometimes feel the urge to teach you what real misfortune is like.

"To see you this way, my delicate beauty, with your

feet in the mud and your eyes turned mistily towards the sky, as if asking for a king, you give the impression of a young frog invoking the ideal. If you despise the harmless King Log, which is who I presently am, as you well know, beware the crane that will chew you up, swallow you down and kill you at his pleasure!

"I might be a poet, but I'm not as gullible as you might think, and if you weary me too often with your *precious* whimpering, I'll treat you like a *wild woman*, or toss you out of the window like an empty bottle."

XII. Crowds

Not everyone is happy rubbing shoulders with the multitude; enjoyment of the crowd is an art; and the capacity to indulge in an orgy of vitality to the detriment of others is given only to someone in whom, in the cradle, a fairy has instilled a taste for costumes and masks, a hatred of home life, and a passion for travel.

Multitude, solitude: equivalent and interchangeable terms for the active and creative poet. He who cannot people his solitude does not know either how to be alone in a bustling crowd.

The poet enjoys the incomparable privilege of being either himself or someone else, as he chooses. Like those wandering souls in search of a body, he enters at will each man's personality. For him alone, all is available, and if certain places appear closed to him, it is because in his eyes they are not worth visiting.

The solitary, pensive stroller derives a singular intoxication from this universal communion. He who can easily embrace the crowd enjoys febrile delights that are denied to the egocentric in their self-imposed isolation, and the lazy, imprisoned like molluscs in their shell. He embraces every profession and assumes all the joys and sorrows that chance offers him.

What men call love is a very modest, limited, and feeble affair when compared to this ineffable orgy, this sacred prostitution of the soul that gives its entire being, all its poetry and charity, to the unforeseen event or the passing stranger.

It is sometimes worth teaching the fortunate of this

Crowds

world, if only to momentarily curb their foolish pride, that there are felicities superior to theirs, more expansive and more refined. Founders of colonies, pastors of the people and missionary priests exiled in faraway places must all know something of these mysterious intoxications; and in the bosom of the vast family their genius has created, they must sometimes laugh at those who pity them for their turbulent lot and their virtuous life.

XIII. Widows

Vauvenargues says that in public parks there are paths that are mainly frequented by defeated ambition, by luckless inventors, frustrated glories, broken hearts, by all those turbulent, closed souls in whom the last sighs of a storm still rumble on, and who retreat far from the insolent gaze of the happy and the idle. These shady retreats are the meeting-places of those defeated by life.

It is especially toward such places that poets and philosophers like to direct their eager hypotheses. For them these are fertile pastures. For if there is one place they disdain to visit, as I have said before, it is where the rich like to congregate for their pleasure. That vacuous hubbub holds no attraction for them. On the contrary, they feel themselves irresistibly drawn towards all that is fragile, destitute, afflicted, orphaned.

The expert eye is never deceived. In those austere, downcast features, those hollow, lustreless eyes, glowing with the last embers of strife, those numerous deep furrows, those slow or hobbling gaits, it discerns at once countless stories of unrequited love, unrecognised devotion, unrewarded endeavours, cold and hunger humbly and silently endured.

Have you ever noticed an impoverished widow seated alone on a park bench? Whether or not they are in mourning, it is easy to recognize them. Besides, there is always something missing in a poor person's grief, an absence of harmony that renders it more upsetting. The poor are constrained to stint on their grief. The rich bear theirs in its entirety.

Which widow is sadder and more poignant, the one

who pulls along a toddler by the hand, with whom she cannot share her thoughts, or the one who is entirely alone? I do not know… I once happened to follow for hours one such woebegone old woman; she was rigid, upright, wrapped in a worn-out shawl, and her whole being exhibited a proud stoicism.

It would seem that she was condemned by sheer solitude to the habits of an old spinster, and the masculine nature of her demeanour added a mysterious piquancy to its austerity. I do not know in what squalid café and in what manner she had partaken of lunch. I followed her to a reading room and watched for a long time as she scanned the gazettes with inquisitive eyes that were once scalded by her tears, for some news of strong personal interest.

Anyway, that afternoon, under a lovely autumn sky, one of those skies from which regrets and memories descend in their droves, she sat on her own in a park, to listen, away from the crowd, to one of those concerts of regimental music so beloved of the people of Paris.

This was no doubt the little indulgence of that innocent (or perhaps purified) old woman, the well-earned consolation for one of those dull, friendless, joyless days, with no one to confide in, that God has inflicted upon her, perhaps for many years now, three hundred and sixty-five times a year.

Another one:

I can never help casting a glance, at least in curiosity if not entirely in sympathy, towards the crowd of social outcasts that gather outside the enclosure at a public concert. The orchestra sends out into the night songs of celebration, triumph, and sensuality. Dresses float and shimmer; glances are exchanged; the idle, weary from doing nothing, shuffle about, feigning nonchalant enjoyment of the music. Here there is nothing but wealth and contentment; nothing that does not breathe and inspire insouciance and the pleasure of taking life as it comes; nothing, except for the sight of that rabble over there pressed up against the outer enclosure, catching, when the wind allows, a few free notes, and watching the glittering splendour within.

It is always of interest to see the gaiety of the rich reflected in the eyes of the poor. But that day, among all those people in their smocks and overalls, I caught sight of a being whose noble air contrasted markedly with all the surrounding triviality.

Here was a tall, majestic woman, so noble in her whole bearing, that I cannot recall having seen her equal in the collections of aristocratic beauties of the past. A fragrance of proud virtue emanated from her whole person. Her face, sad and emaciated, was in perfect accord with the mourning clothes that she wore. She too, like the populace with which she mingled yet to which she paid no attention, gazed profoundly into that luminous world, while gently moving her head in time with the music.

Singular vision! "Surely", I said to myself, "poverty such as this, if poverty it is, need not admit to vulgar frugality; such a noble countenance tells me so. Why then does she choose to remain in surroundings where she stands out so strikingly?"

But on passing close by her out of curiosity, I thought

Widows

I divined the reason. She was holding the hand of a child, who like her was dressed in black. Modest as the entry cost would have been, it was perhaps enough to pay for one of the little one's needs, or maybe a little knickknack to play with.

And she will have returned home, musing, dreaming, alone, always alone; for a child is boisterous, selfish, lacks gentleness or patience, and unlike a dog or a cat he cannot be a confidant in times of solitary grief.

XIV. The Old Entertainer

The excited holiday crowd fanned out in all directions. It was one of those celebrations that clowns, acrobats, animal tamers and itinerant stallholders have long relied on to compensate for the year's leaner times.

On days like this it seems to me that people forget everything, their sorrows and their labours; they revert to childhood. For the youngsters it is a day's holiday, the horror of school postponed for twenty-four hours; for the adults it's a truce agreed with the malignant forces of life, a brief respite from all-consuming conflict and struggle.

Even the man of the world and the man occupied by spiritual pursuits find it difficult to avoid the influence of this popular jubilee. They absorb involuntarily their share of this carefree atmosphere. For my part, as a true Parisian, I never miss the opportunity to visit the many stalls that spring up on these festive occasions.

In truth there was a formidable rivalry between them: they yelled, bellowed, and howled. There was a mixture of shouting, trumpet blasts and exploding rockets. The red-tails and buffoons contorted their swarthy faces, lined by the wind, the rain, and the sun; with the self-assurance of actors confident in their performance, they tossed out wisecracks and pleasantries with a comical effect as solid and predictable as that of Molière. Strong men, proud of their enormous limbs, with foreheads and skulls like orangutans, lounged augustly in their singlets, laundered the previous day for the occasion. The dancers, lovely as fairies or princesses, leapt and caprioled beneath the glow of the lanterns that filled their skirts with iridescence.

The Old Entertainer

All was light, dust, cries, joy, and uproar; some spent while others earned, and both were equally happy. Children tugged at their mothers' skirts to obtain some sugary treat, or climbed up onto their fathers' shoulders to get a better view of a magician dazzling like a god. And everywhere there floated, transcending all other odours, an aroma of fried food, which seemed to be the incense of this festival.

At the far end of a row of kiosks, as though out of shame he had exiled himself from all this splendour, I saw a poor old entertainer, stooped, haggard, decrepit, a ruin of a man, leaning against one of the posts of his shack, a hovel more wretched than that of the lowest degenerate, and whose squalor the melting and smoking remains of two candles illuminated only too well.

Everywhere was joy, wealth, and indulgence; everywhere the guarantee of food for the next day; everywhere the frenetic explosion of vitality. Here there was absolute penury, disguised, to amplify the horror, in comical rags to which necessity, rather than art, provided the contrast. That poor wretch did not laugh, he did not weep, he did not dance he did not sing of joy or sorrow; he asked for nothing. He was silent and motionless. He had given up, abdicated. His destiny was set.

But what a profound, unforgettable gaze he directed towards the crowd and the lights, the moving tide of which stopped but a few feet away from his abject squalor! I felt my throat gripped by the terrible hand of hysteria, and my eyes were clouded by obstinate tears that refused to fall.

The Old Entertainer

What was I to do? Was there any point in asking the unfortunate fellow what curiosities, what wonders he had to show me in this nauseous gloom, behind his shredded curtain? To tell the truth, I dared not; and, although the reason for my timidity may make you laugh, I will admit that I feared humiliating him. Anyway, I had just decided to place some money on one of his planks as I walked by, hoping that he would understand my intention, when I was swept far from him by some disturbance or other that caused the crowd to suddenly surge forward.

And on my way home, obsessed by this vision, I sought to analyse my sudden sadness, saying to myself: I have just seen the image of an old man of letters who has outlived the generation he had so brilliantly entertained; an old poet without friends, family, or children, demeaned by his poverty and the ingratitude of the public, and whose shack an indifferent world no longer cares to enter!

XV. Cake

I was on my travels. The landscape in which I found myself was one of irresistible grandeur and nobility, and something of it undoubtedly entered my soul. My thoughts fluttered upon the lightness of the atmosphere; vulgar passions like hatred and profane love now seemed as far away as the clouds that cascaded into the depths of the chasms beneath my feet; my soul seemed as vast and pure as the dome of the sky that enveloped me; the memory of earthly things that entered my heart were faint and diminished, like the tinkling of bells of indiscernible cattle grazing on a distant mountainside. Above the peaceful little lake, rendered black by its immense depth, there sometimes passed the shadow of a cloud, like the cloak of an airborne giant traversing the sky. And I recall that this solemn and rare sensation, caused by a great, perfectly silent movement, imbued me with a mixture of joy and fear. In short, I felt, thanks to the captivating beauty around me, at perfect peace with myself and the universe; indeed, my state of supreme bliss rendered me oblivious to the evils of the world, and I no longer found so absurd those journals which claim that man is born good; when, stubborn matter renewing its demands, my thoughts turned to relieving the fatigue and assuaging the hunger caused by so long a climb. I took from of my pocket a large piece of bread, a leather cup, and a flask of a certain potion that pharmacists used to sell to tourists at the time, to be mixed as required with melted snow.

I was calmly slicing my bread when a slight noise made me look up. Before me stood a swarthy, ragged, dishevelled little being, whose hollow eyes, feral yet imploring, were devouring the piece of bread. And I heard him sigh with a low, hoarse voice, the word: cake!

Cake

I could not help laughing on hearing the appellation with which he wished to honour my pallid loaf, and I cut him a generous slice, which I offered him. Slowly he approached, never taking his eyes off the object of his desire; then, seizing the piece with his hand, he hastily retreated, as if he feared that my offer had not been sincere, or that I already regretted it.

But there and then he was promptly floored by a second little savage who seemed to have appeared from nowhere, and who so perfectly resembled the first that he might have been his twin. Together they rolled about on the ground, fighting over the precious prey, neither apparently willing to give up half to his brother. The first one, incensed, grasped the second one by his hair; the latter sank his teeth into the other's ear, and spat out a bloody little piece of it with a splendid colloquial expletive. The legitimate owner of the cake tried to sink his little claws into the usurper's eyes; in his turn the latter used all his strength to strangle his adversary with one hand, while with the other attempting to slip the prize of the combat into his pocket. But, reinvigorated by despair, the loser got back on his feet and sent his conqueror reeling to the ground with a head butt to the stomach. What is the point of recounting a gruesome brawl that in truth lasted far longer than their immature stamina would have seemed to predict? The cake travelled from hand to hand and kept changing from one pocket to the other; but alas! it also changed in size; and when at last, worn out, gasping for breath, and covered in blood, they stopped because they could carry on no longer, there was, truth to tell, nothing left to fight over; the piece of bread had disappeared, scattered into crumbs that resembled the grains of sand with which

Cake

they were intermingled.

For me, this spectacle had clouded the landscape, and the blissful serenity in which my soul had rejoiced before observing those little men had completely disappeared; I remained downcast for quite some time, telling myself repeatedly: "There is, then, a wonderful country where bread is called cake, a delicacy so rare that nothing else is needed to provoke an outright fratricidal war!"

XVI. The Clock

The Chinese can tell the time in the eyes of a cat.

One day a missionary, strolling through the suburbs of Nanking, realised that he had forgotten his watch, and asked a little boy what time it was.

The urchin of the Celestial Empire hesitated at first; then, on second thoughts, he replied, "I'll let you know." Moments later he reappeared, carrying an enormous cat, and looking, as they say, into the whites of its eyes, he declared without hesitation: "It's almost noon." Which was correct.

For my part, if I incline myself towards my beautiful Féline, so well named, who is at once the honour of her sex, the pride of my heart, and the redolence of my spirit, be it night or day, in bright light or deep shade, in the depths of her adorable eyes I always see the hour distinctly, always the same, a vast, solemn hour, as great as space, without divisions into minutes or seconds, a motionless hour that is not marked on any clock, yet light as a sigh, swift as a glance.

And should some busybody come to disturb me while my gaze rests upon this delightful timepiece, or some cynical and intolerant Genie, some Demon of the inopportune, come to me and say, "What are you looking at there so intently? What do you seek in the eyes of this creature? Do you see the time there, prodigal and indolent mortal?", I should reply forthwith: "Yes, I see the time; it is Eternity!"

Is this not, madame, a commendable conceit, as pretentious as yourself? To be honest, I have had such pleasure embroidering this gratuitous frivolity, that I shall ask for nothing in return.

XVII. A Hemisphere in her Hair

Long, long may I inhale the fragrance of your hair, sink my face into it like a thirsting man into the waters of a spring, and ruffle it with my hand like a scented kerchief, sending memories out into the air.

If only you knew all that I can see, sense, and hear in your hair! My soul floats upon its fragrance just as the souls of other men drift upon music.

Your hair enshrouds a dream, filled with sails and masts; it encompasses great seas whose monsoon winds carry me off to enchanting climes, where the vastness is of a deeper blue, where the air is scented by fruits, leaves, and human skin.

In the ocean of your hair I see a harbour, alive with melancholy song, robust men of every nation, and myriad vessels whose exquisite, detailed shapes are silhouetted against the immensity of a sky where eternal warmth resides.

As I caress your hair, I relive the languor of long hours reclining on a divan in the stateroom of a splendid ship, rocked by the barely perceptible swell of the mooring and surrounded by vases of flowers and pitchers of refreshing water.

In the glowing hearth of your hair, I inhale the odour of tobacco infused with opium and sugar; in the night of your hair, I see the resplendence of the infinite azure of the tropics; on the downy shores of your hair, I am intoxicated by odours of tar, musk, and coconut oil.

Let me sink my teeth into your thick black tresses. When I savour your supple, rebellious locks, it is as if I am dining on memories.

XVIII. Invitation to a Journey

There is a wondrous land, a land of Cockaigne, it is said, that I dream of visiting with one I have loved for so long. A strange land, shrouded in our northern mists, that one might call the Orient of the West, the Cathay of Europe, so freely does a warm and capricious fantasy flourish there, so patiently and wisely depicted in its delicate vegetation.

Truly a land of Cockaigne, where all is beautiful, rich, tranquil, harmonious; where luxury and order are happily wed; where life is opulent and sweet to inhale; whence disorder, tumult and the unforeseen are banished; where bliss is wedded to silence; where even the cuisine is at once poetic, rich and exciting; where everything is just like you, my darling angel.

You know the feverish sickness that descends upon us on days of dark despond, that nostalgia for an unknown land, that torment of curiosity? There is a place that is just like you, where all is beautiful, rich, tranquil, and harmonious, where fantasy has built and adorned a Cathay of the west, where life is sweet to breathe, where happiness is wedded to silence. That is where we must go to live, that is where we must go to die!

Yes, that is where we must go to breathe, to dream and to draw out the hours with an infinity of sensations. A musician once wrote the *Invitation to the Waltz*; who will compose the *Invitation to a Journey* that one could offer to the woman one loves, to one's chosen sister?

Yes, it is in such surroundings that it would be so good to dwell, — there, where the unhurried hours contain more thoughts, where the clocks chime contentment with

Invitation to a Journey

a more profound and meaningful solemnity.

On gleaming panels, or on opulent, dark, gilded leathers, are discreetly disposed serene, profound paintings, like the souls of the artists who created them. The setting sun, that so richly emblazons the dining room or the parlour, is screened by beautiful fabrics or by high, finely wrought windows that are divided by lead beadings into numerous sections. The cabinets are huge, curious, bizarre, equipped with locks and loaded with secrets like refined souls. The mirrors, the bronzes, the fabrics, the silverware, and the ceramics perform for the eyes a silent, mysterious symphony, and from all things, from the gaps in the drawers to the folds of the curtains, there escapes a rare perfume, a *come-back* memento of Sumatra that is, as it were, the soul of the dwelling.

Truly a land of Cockaigne, I say, where all is opulent, spotless, gleaming, like a clear conscience, resplendent kitchenware, finely wrought gold, or richly coloured gemstones! The earth's treasures abound there, as in the home of a diligent man who has prospered well from all the world has to offer. An exceptional land, superior to others as Art is to Nature, where the latter is enhanced by dreams, improved, embellished, reshaped.

May those alchemists of horticulture never tire in their mission to constantly push the boundaries of their happiness! Let them offer prizes of sixty or a hundred thousand florins to anyone who can resolve their ambitious problems! For my part, I have found my *black tulip* and my *blue dahlia*!

Incomparable flower, rediscovered tulip, allegorical

dahlia, it is there, is it not, in that beautiful, calm, and dreamlike land, that you must live and prosper? Would you not be framed within your own analogy, and see yourself, as the mystics would say, in your own *correspondence*?

Dreams! always dreams! And the more ambitious and discerning the soul, the greater the divide between dream and reality. Every man has his own dose of natural opium, endlessly secreted and renewed, and from birth to death, how many hours can we count that are filled with true joy, with successful and decisive action? Will we ever know, will we ever be part of this picture that my spirit has painted, this picture that is in your image?

These treasures, these furnishings, this luxury, this order, these perfumes, these miraculous flowers, all resemble you. The great rivers and peaceful canals, they too resemble you; and those great ships that sail upon them, laden with riches, and from which rise the monotonous chants of the crew, these are my thoughts that slumber and float upon your breast. You steer them gently to the sea of Infinity, as you mirror the sky's depths in the pure beauty of your soul; —and when, fatigued by the ocean's swell and laden with produce from the East, they return to their native port, they are still my thoughts, returning enriched from Infinity to you.

XIX. The Poor Boy's Toy

I would like to propose an innocent diversion. There are so few that are not culpable!

When you go out for a morning stroll around the city streets, fill your pockets with cheap little gadgets, such as a cardboard punch worked by a string, a blacksmith beating an anvil, or a rider on a horse with a whistle for a tail, and outside the cafes or under the trees, offer them as gifts to the penniless urchins that you meet. You will see their eyes grow inordinately wide. At first, they will not dare take them, doubting their good fortune. Then their hands will eagerly seize the gift, and they will quickly make off, like cats that turn tail to devour at a safe distance the morsel you have given them, having learned to be wary of humans.

On a highway, behind the iron gates of a grand garden, at the far end of which was a fine white mansion bathed in sunlight, there was a handsome, bright-eyed little boy, dressed in those country clothes that are so fashionably stylish.

Luxury, freedom from care, and habitual exposure to wealth render these children so attractive that you would think they are made from a different mould than children from a poor family.

Beside him on the grass lay a splendid toy, as spruce as its master, glossy, gilded, dressed in a burgundy outfit, and covered with plumes and glass beads. But the child was not playing with his favourite toy, and here is what he was looking at:

On the other side of the gate, on the road, among the

The Poor Boy's Toy

thistles and nettles, there was another child, scruffy, sickly, grimy, one of those outcast urchins in whom an impartial eye might perceive beauty, just as the eye of a connoisseur might detect a work of art hidden beneath layers of industrial varnish, if it could erase the abhorrent patina of penury.

Through those symbolic bars separating two worlds, the public road and the private estate, the poor child was showing the rich child his own toy, which the latter scrutinised eagerly as if it were some rare and mysterious object. Now, this toy that the little urchin was prodding and shaking inside a makeshift cage, was a live rat! The parents, for reasons of frugality no doubt, had culled the toy from life itself.

And the two children laughed together fraternally, with teeth of equal whiteness.

XX. The Fairies' Gifts

It was the Grand Assembly of Fairies, convened for the purpose of allocating gifts to all the new-born babies of the past twenty-four hours.

These ancient and capricious Sisters of Destiny, these bizarre Mothers of joy and sorrow, were all quite different from one another: some appeared sombre and sullen, while others seemed spirited and mischievous; some were young, and had always been young; others were old, and had always been old.

All the fathers who believed in Fairies were there, each carrying his new-born in his arms.

The Gifts, Faculties, good Fortunes, and invincible Circumstances were amassed beside the tribunal, like prizes on the stage at a prize-giving. What was different here was that the Gifts were not a reward for effort but, on the contrary, they were a grace accorded to someone who had not yet lived, a grace that could determine his destiny and become as much the source of his misery as of his happiness.

The poor Fairies were kept very busy, for the crowd of petitioners was substantial, and the intermediate world, situated between man and God, is subject just as we are to the terrible law of Time and its infinite progeny, the Days, the Hours, the Minutes, and the Seconds.

In truth, they were as flustered as ministers in session, or the pawnbrokers of the *Mont-de-Piété* when a national holiday allows free redemptions. I suspect that from time to time they were watching the hands of the clock as impatiently as human judges might when they

The Fairies' Gifts

have been sitting since early morning and are now dreaming of their dinner, their family, and their beloved slippers. If, in supernatural justice, there is an element of expediency and inconsistency, we should not be surprised that the same is sometimes also true when it comes to human justice. We ourselves, in that case, would be unjust judges.

Consequently, some blunders were committed that day that one might consider bizarre if prudence, rather than whim, were the distinctive, eternal character of Fairies.

So, the power of attracting wealth like a magnet was awarded to the sole heir of a wealthy family who, being endowed with no sense of charity, nor with any desire for life's more discernible benefits, was to find himself in later life hugely embarrassed by his millions.

Likewise, the love of Beauty and the Power of Poetry were awarded to the son of a miserable pauper, a quarryman by trade, who could in no way stimulate the faculties or support the needs of his deplorable offspring.

I should have mentioned that the allocation, on these solemn occasions, is without appeal, and that no gift may be refused.

The Fairies all rose, believing their duty fulfilled, for there remained no more gifts, no more largesse to bestow on this human riffraff, when one fine fellow, a poor little shopkeeper, I believe, stood up, and seizing the nearest Fairy by her multi-coloured gossamer dress, cried:

"Hey, Madame! You're forgetting us! There's still my

The Fairies' Gifts

little one! I don't want to have come all this way for nothing!"

The Fairy might well have been embarrassed, as there was nothing left. However, she remembered just in time that there is a law, well-known though rarely applied, in the supernatural world inhabited by those intangible deities, friends to humans and often obliged to accommodate their emotions, such as Fairies, Gnomes, Salamanders, Sylphids, Sylphs, Nixes, Undines and Sprites. I am talking about the law that gives Fairies, in a case like this when the supply of prizes is exhausted, the power to award just one extra gift, provided of course that she has sufficient imagination to create it on the spot.

So the good Fairy replied, with a self-assurance that befitted her rank: "I give your son . . .I give him… the Gift of pleasing!"

"Pleasing? What do you mean, pleasing? Why pleasing?" asked the indignant little shopkeeper, who was no doubt one of those all-too-common reasoners who are incapable of elevating their intellect to the logic of the Absurd.

"Because! because!" replied the indignant Fairy, turning her back on him; and re-joining her peers, she said: "What do you think of this pretentious little Frenchman who wants an explanation for everything, and who, having obtained for his son the best prize of all, still dares to question and debate the undebatable?"

XXI. Temptations

or Eros, Plutus, and Glory

Last night, two superb Satans and an equally remarkable She-Devil ascended the mysterious stairway by which Hell mounts an attack on the helplessness of a sleeping man to secretly communicate with him. And they stood before me in all their glory, as if on a rostrum. An infernal splendour emanated from those three individuals, as they stood out against the dense background of the night. They displayed such an august and dominant air that at first I mistook the three of them for genuine Gods.

The first Satan's face was of ambiguous gender, and the contours of his body had the rotundity of an ancient Bacchus. His beautiful, languid eyes, with their shadowy, uncertain colour, resembled violets still laden with the heavy tears of a storm, and his half-opened lips were like hot censers, exhaling the fine odour of a perfumery; and with each sigh, musk-laden insects glowed and fluttered in the heat of his breath.

Around his purple tunic was wound, like a girdle, a glistening serpent which, its head raised, turned its incandescent eyes languorously towards him. From this living girdle there hung alternately vials of sinister liquids, gleaming knives, and surgical instruments. In his right hand he held another vial whose contents were of a luminous red, bearing a label with these bizarre words: "Drink, this is my blood, a perfect cordial"; in his left hand was a violin which he doubtless used to sing of his pleasures and sorrows, and to spread the contagion of his madness on sabbath nights.

From his delicate ankles there hung a few links of a

Temptations

broken gold chain, and when the resulting discomfort caused him to look down towards the ground, he proudly admired his toenails, shining and polished like finely cut gemstones.

He looked at me with inconsolably plaintive eyes from which there flowed an insidious intoxication, and he said to me in a singing voice: "If you wish, if you wish, I will make you the lord of souls, and you will be the master of living matter, more so than a sculptor is of his clay; and you will discover the ever- renascent pleasure of escaping from yourself to engage with the souls of others, until you confuse them with your own."

And I replied, "No thank you! I have no need of those dregs of humanity who, no doubt, are of no more value than my own poor self. Although I am somewhat ashamed of my memories, I do not wish to forget anything either; and even if I did not already know you, you old monster, your mysterious silverware, your ambivalent vials, and the chains that entangle your feet are symbols that explain quite clearly the drawbacks of being your friend. Keep your gifts."

The second Satan had neither that tragic yet smiling air, nor those fine, ingratiating manners, nor that delicate and perfumed beauty. He was an enormous man with a rotund, eyeless face, whose huge paunch overhung his thighs, and whose entire skin was gilded and illustrated, as if tattooed, with a host of little moving figures representing the numerous forms of universal misery. There were scrawny little men hanging from nails; gaunt, misshapen little gnomes with imploring eyes that begged more effectively for alms than their trembling hands; and ageing mothers with sickly infants clinging to their dried

Temptations

up breasts. There were many more besides.

The fat Satan was beating his enormous paunch, from which there resonated a prolonged jangling of metal, culminating in a vague chorus of moaning human voices. And he let out a loud, imbecilic laugh that revealed his rotten teeth, as men the world over are wont to do when they have dined too well.

And he said to me: "I can give you what obtains all things, is worth all things, and takes the place of all things!" And he beat his huge belly, whence the sonorous echo was like a critique of his vulgar words.

I turned away in disgust and replied: "I derive no pleasure from someone else's misery, and I do not want wealth that is tainted with all the misfortunes depicted like a tapestry on your skin."

As for the She-Devil, I would be lying if I did not admit to finding her strangely alluring at first sight. To define that allure, I cannot think of a better comparison than that of those beautiful women who are past their prime but have ceased growing any older, and whose beauty retains the penetrating alchemy of a ruin. She seemed at once both imperious and ungainly, and her eyes, though despondent, still possessed a fascinating energy. What struck me most was the mystery in her voice that reminded me of the most exquisite *contralti*, together with the huskiness of a throat that was regularly bathed in alcohol.

"Do you want to know my power?" said the false goddess in her incongruously enchanting voice. "Listen."

Temptations

And she put to her lips a huge trumpet, beribboned like a tin whistle with the titles of all the newspapers of the world, and through that trumpet she called out my name, which travelled through space with the sound of a hundred thousand explosions and reverberated back to me like an echo from the most distant planet.

"Strewth!" I said, half transfixed, "that *is* something! But on closer examination of the beguiling virago, I seemed to recall having seen her somewhere, drinking with some scoundrels of my acquaintance; and the rasping sound of the brass conveyed to my ears the vague reminiscence of a prostituted trumpet.

I therefore replied, with the utmost disdain: "Begone! I have no desire to marry the mistress of certain people I'd rather not name."

Indeed, I was entitled to feel proud of my resolute abrogation. But unfortunately I awoke, and all my strength abandoned me. "Truly," I told myself, "I must really have been sound asleep to have shown such misgivings. Ah, if only they could come back now that I'm awake, I wouldn't be so squeamish!"

And I called aloud to them, begging them to forgive me, offering to dishonour myself as often as necessary in order to deserve their favours; but I had apparently sorely offended them, for they have never returned.

XXII. Evening Twilight

Daylight is fading. Immense solace descends upon the poor souls wearied by the day's toil; and their thoughts take on the gentle, indistinct colours of the twilight.

But from the mountaintop, through the translucent evening haze, a great cacophony of discordant cries reaches my balcony, transformed by space into a doleful harmony, like that of the rising tide or an impending storm.

Who are those unfortunates that evening cannot assuage, and who, like owls, see the coming of night as a cue for ritual? That sinister howling reaches us from the dark asylum perched on the mountainside, and as I smoke and contemplate the tranquillity of the immense valley, dotted with houses whose every window proclaims, "Here is now peace; here is the joy of family life!", I can, when the wind blows from up there, temper my bewildered reaction to this imitation of the harmonies of hell.

Twilight can excite the feeble-minded. I recall that I once had two friends whom twilight would render very poorly. One of them would forget any notion of friendship and civility, brutishly abusing anyone he encountered. I once saw him throw a perfectly good chicken back at a waiter, believing he could see in it some sort of insulting hieroglyph. Eventide, the precursor to intense pleasures, for him would tarnish the most mouth-watering of delights.

The other, an ambitious failure, would become, as daylight faded, increasingly bitter, sombre, and annoying. Considerate and convivial during the day,

Evening Twilight

he would become implacable at dusk; and it was not only upon others but also upon himself that his crepuscular folly would be visited.

The first one died insane, incapable of recognising his wife and his child; the second still carries within him a burden of constant unease, and even were he to be favoured with all the honours that republics and princes can bestow, I believe that the twilight hours would still ignite within him a burning desire for imaginary distinctions. Night, which imparted darkness to their spirit, brings light into mine; and though it is not uncommon to see the same cause produce two opposite effects, I am still both intrigued and alarmed by it.

O night, O refreshing darkness! For me you are the signal for an internal feast, you are my redemption from anguish! In the solitude of the plain or the stone labyrinths of the capital, in the twinkling of the stars or the glow of the streetlamps, you are the pyrotechnics of the goddess Libertas!

Twilight, how sweet and tender you are! The rose-tinted rays that still loiter on the horizon, like the death throes of the day under night's victorious dominion, the blazing candelabras that cast opaque red stains on the last glories of the setting sun, the heavy curtains that an invisible hand draws from the depths of the Orient, mimic all the complex feelings that vie with each other in a man's heart during the solemn hours of his life.

Picture one of those strange robes worn by dancers: beneath a dark, transparent gauze we discern the muted splendour of a dazzling skirt, like past delights that

Evening Twilight

transpierce present darkness; and the flickering stars of gold and silver with which it is bespangled are the flames of fantasy that only appear in the profound melancholy of the Night.

XXIII. Solitude

A well-meaning journalist tells me that solitude is bad for a man; and in support of his thesis he cites, as do all non-believers, the words of the Church Fathers.

I know that the Devil is wont to frequent arid places, and that the Spirit of murder and depravity is mysteriously ignited in the wilderness. But it might be possible that this solitude is only dangerous for the idle, desultory soul who peoples it with his passions and his fantasies.

It is certain that a blowhard, whose supreme joy consists in sermonising from a pulpit or a stage, would be at serious risk of going raving mad on Robinson's island. I do not require of my journalist the courageous qualities of a Crusoe, but I do ask him not to lay down the law to those who love solitude and mystery.

There are, among our chattering classes, some individuals who would not recoil from the death penalty so long as they could deliver a verbose diatribe from the scaffold, without fear that Santerre's drums would interrupt them in an untimely manner.

I do not pity them, for I suppose that their oratorical effusions procure for them pleasures equal to those that others derive from silence and self-communion; but I do despise them.

I desire above all that my blasted journalist would let me amuse myself in my own way. "So you never feel," he asks me, in a most apostolic nasal tone, "the need to share your pleasures?" Do you see his subtle envy! He knows that I disdain his pleasures, so he comes and pokes

Solitude

his nose into mine, the tiresome killjoy!

"That unfortunate inability to be alone!" says La Bruyère somewhere or other, as if to shame all those who rush to lose themselves in the crowd, probably afraid that they could not tolerate themselves on their own.

"Almost all our woes stem from our inability to remain in our own room," said another sage, Pascal, I believe, summoning thus to the retreat of self-communion all those hysterics who seek happiness in movement and in a prostitution that I might call *fraternalism*, were I to speak the fine language of my century.

XXIV. Plans

He said to himself, as he wandered across the lonely expanse of parkland: "How lovely she would be in an intricate, gorgeous stately gown, descending, in the ambience of a splendid evening, the marble steps of a palace overlooking grand lawns and lakes! For she has the natural air of a princess."

Walking down a street a little later, he stopped outside a print shop, and, spotting in a cardboard box an engraving of a tropical landscape, he said to himself: "No! It is not in a palace that I would wish to share her precious life. We would not be at home there! Besides, those walls covered with gold would not leave any space to hang her picture; in those solemn galleries there are no intimate corners. Clearly, this is the place to live in order to cultivate my life's dream."

And casting a critical eye over every detail of the engraving, he resumed his musing: "By the seashore, a splendid log cabin, surrounded by all those strange, luminous trees whose names I've forgotten… outside, an intoxicating, enigmatic fragrance… inside, a powerful perfume of rose and musk… further off, beyond our little domain, mast-tops rocked by the waves… around us, beyond our room, lit by a roseate glow filtered through the blinds, adorned with cool matting and intoxicating flowers, with rare Portuguese rococo chairs made of dense dark wood (where she would serenely rest, gently fanned, smoking tobacco with a hint of opium!), and beyond the veranda, the noise of birds inebriated by the light, and the chattering of little native girls, and at night, to serve as accompaniment to my dreams, the plaintive song of musical trees, those melancholy filaos: Yes, indeed, that's exactly the décor I was seeking. What

Plans

would I want with palaces?"

And further on, as he walked down a wide avenue, he saw a well-kept little inn where, from a window decked with gaily coloured calico curtains, there leaned two laughing faces. And straight away he said to himself: "My thoughts must indeed have a wanderlust to go searching so far afield for what is so close to me. Pleasure and happiness are to be found in a nearby inn, a chanced-upon inn replete with delights. A roaring fire, garish tableware, a passable supper, cheap wine, and a generous bed with rough but clean sheets: what could be better?"

And on returning home alone, at that hour when the counsels of Wisdom are no longer stifled by the buzz of exterior life, he said to himself: "I have today, in my fancy, had three homes in which I found equal pleasure. Why force my body to move elsewhere when my soul can travel so freely? And why bother to go ahead with one's plans when the plan itself is enjoyment enough?"

XXV. Lovely Dorothea

The sun beats down on the town with its awesome perpendicular light; the sand is dazzling and the sea shimmers. The dazed world succumbs cravenly to its siesta, a siesta that is a kind of pleasurable death in which the sleeper, still half awake, tastes the delights of his own extinction.

But Dorothea, strong and proud as the sun, walks along the deserted street, the only living soul at that hour beneath the vast azure sky, creating a striking black silhouette against the light.

She continues on her way, languidly swaying her slim torso above her ample hips. Her close-fitting silk dress, in a light shade of pink, contrasts sharply with the darkness of her skin and sets off perfectly the contour of her waist, the hollow of her back and her pointed breasts.

Her red parasol, filtering the sunlight, projects a patch of crimson onto her dark face.

The weight of her abundant hair, almost blue in colour, draws her delicate head backwards, lending her a triumphant and languorous air. Heavy glass pendants twitter secretly on her dainty ears.

Now and then the sea breeze lifts the hem of her flowing skirts, revealing an exquisite silken leg; and the foot, rivalling the feet of those marble goddesses that Europe confines to its museums, faithfully imprints its form in the fine sand. For Dorothea is so prodigiously coquette that the pleasure of being admired takes precedence over her pride in being emancipated, and, though she is free, she still goes barefoot.

Lovely Dorothea

She proceeds thus, harmoniously, happy to be alive and wearing a subtle smile, as if she could see in the distance a mirror reflecting her demeanour and her comeliness. At the hour when even dogs moan in pain beneath the blistering sun, what powerful motive inspires the carefree Dorothea to venture forth in this way, beautiful and cool as bronze?

Why has she left her demurely arranged little cabin, where the flowers and mattings make a perfect boudoir at so little expense; where she so loves to sit and comb her hair, smoking or gazing into her mirror while fanning herself with her great feather fans, while the sea, lapping at the nearby shore, provides a powerful, hypnotic accompaniment to her ethereal musings, and the iron cooking-pot, in which there simmers a stew of crab with rice and saffron, wafts its enticing odours from the terrace outside?

Perhaps she plans a tryst with some young officer who, on distant shores, has heard his comrades tell of the renowned Dorothea. She will surely beg him, simple creature that she is, to tell her all about the Opera Ball, and ask if one can go there barefoot, as to the Sunday dances where even old Kaffir women become intoxicated and frenzied with joy; and also whether the beautiful ladies of Paris are all more beautiful than she is.

Dorothea is admired and cossetted by everyone, and her happiness would be complete if only she were not obliged to save every penny she can to buy the freedom of her little sister, who is just eleven years old but already mature, and so beautiful! Kind-hearted Dorothea will doubtless succeed, for the child's master is too miserly to understand any beauty other than that of money!

XXVI. The Eyes of the Poor

Ah, so you want to know why I hate you today. It will doubtless be harder for you to understand than for me to explain; for you are, I believe, the finest example of female intransigence that anyone could meet.

We had spent a long day together that to me had seemed short. We had promised one another that all our thoughts would be shared between the two of us, and that our two souls would henceforth become one; —a dream that is after all in no way original except that, though dreamed of by all men, no one has ever attained it.

That evening, feeling a little tired, you wanted to stop at a new café on the corner of a new boulevard that was still piled high with rubble but already gloriously displayed its unfinished splendour. The café was ablaze. The gaslight burned with all the fervour of a premiere, casting its dazzling light on the whiteness of the walls, the resplendent array of mirrors, the gold of the ornaments and cornices, the plump-cheeked page-boys pulled along by dogs on leashes, the laughing ladies with falcons perched on their wrists, the nymphs and goddesses carrying fruits, pâtés and wildfowl on their heads, the Hebes and the Ganymedes proffering little jars of *crème parfait* or a colourful obelisk of assorted sorbets; all of history and mythology pandering to gluttony.

Directly in front of us, in the street, stood a fellow of about forty, with a wearied expression and a greying beard, holding a little boy by the hand and carrying in his other arm a tiny child too feeble to walk. He was playing nursemaid, and had brought his children out to take the evening air. All were dressed in rags. Those three faces bore extremely serious expressions, and those six eyes gazed intently at the café in equal wonderment, but nuanced according to their age.

The father's eyes said: "How beautiful it is! How beautiful it is! It's as if all the gold in our poor world has found its way onto these walls." The little boy's eyes said: "How beautiful it is! How beautiful it is! But this is a place where only people who are not like us can go." As for the tiny child's eyes, they were too fascinated to express anything other than a naïve and profound joy.

Songwriters say that pleasure is good for the soul and softens the heart. The song was right that evening, in my case. Not only was I moved by this family of eyes, but I felt a little ashamed of our glasses and carafes that were so much bigger than our thirst. I turned my gaze toward yours, my love, to read my thoughts there; I plunged my eyes deeply into yours, so beautiful and so strangely soft, into your green eyes, inhabited by Caprice and inspired by the Moon; then you said to me: "Those people are insufferable, with their eyes as wide as coach gates! Can't you ask the head waiter to get them away from here?"

How hard it is to understand one another, my angel. Thought is incommunicable, even between people who love one another!

XXVII. A Heroic Death

Fancioulle was an admirable clown, and almost like a friend to the Prince. But for persons who are condemned by their status to buffoonery, serious things can have a fatal attraction, and, though it may seem odd that ideas of patriotism and liberty should despotically take hold of an actor's mind, Fancioulle became part of a conspiracy initiated by certain discontented noblemen.

There exist everywhere upstanding men prepared to denounce those individuals of perverse disposition who seek to depose princes, and to bring about, without consultation, a restructuring of society. The noblemen in question were arrested, together with Fancioulle, and faced certain death.

I am willing to believe that the Prince was almost sorry to find his favourite actor among the rebels. The Prince was neither better nor worse than any other prince; but an excessive sensibility rendered him, in many cases, more cruel and despotic than all his peers. A passionate lover of the fine arts, as well as an excellent connoisseur, he had an insatiable appetite for self-indulgence. Somewhat indifferent regarding men and morals, himself a true artist, the only dangerous enemy he knew was Ennui, and the bizarre efforts that he made to flee or to vanquish that worldly tyrant would certainly have earned him, from a rigorous historian, the epithet of 'monster', had it been permitted, in his dominions, to write anything which did not tend exclusively to pleasure, or to astonishment, one of the subtlest forms of pleasure. The great misfortune of this Prince was that he never had a theatre vast enough for his genius. There are young Neros who are stifled by limits that are too narrow, and whose name and generosity will always be

A Heroic Death

unknown to future generations. Careless Providence had accorded this one faculties greater than his estates.

Suddenly word got out that the sovereign wanted to pardon all the conspirators; and the origin of this rumour was the announcement of a great spectacle in which Fancioulle was to play one of his principal roles, and at which, it was said, even the condemned nobles would be present, an obvious sign, according to superficial minds, of the generous tendencies of the offended Prince.

On the part of a man so naturally and spontaneously eccentric, anything was possible, even virtue, even clemency, especially if he might be hoping to find therein some unexpected pleasure. But for those who, like me, had been able to penetrate further into the depths of this sick and curious soul, it was infinitely more likely that the Prince wanted to assess the value of the acting talents of a man condemned to death. He would take advantage of the occasion to perform an extremely interesting physical experiment and establish to what extent the habitual faculties of an artist could be altered or modified by the extraordinary situation in which he found himself. Beyond that, did there exist in his soul a decided intention of clemency? It is a question that has never been answered.

The great day having at last arrived, that little court displayed all its pomp, and it would be difficult to imagine, without having seen it, all the splendour that the privileged class of a minor state with its modest assets can exhibit for a truly extravagant occasion. Today it was doubly so, due to both the magical luxury on display and the mysterious moral interest that was attached to it.

A Heroic Death

Monsieur Fancioulle excelled above all in roles that were either silent or with few words, which is often the main part in one of those allegorical dramas whose aim is to represent symbolically the mystery of life. He came on stage casually and with perfect ease, which served to enhance, in the minds of the noble public, the idea of gentleness and forgiveness.

When we say of an actor: "This is a good actor," we are using an expression which implies that beneath the character being played we can still divine the actor, the art, the effort, the will. Now, if an actor should manage to become, relative to the character he is assigned to portray, what the finest statues of antiquity would be if they miraculously came to life as animated, walking, seeing beings, in relation to the general and confused concept of beauty, that would be, without doubt, something singularly and wholly unexpected. Fancioulle was, that evening, a perfect idealisation, which it was impossible not to suppose living, possible, real. The buffoon strode up and down, laughing, weeping, convulsing, with an indestructible halo around his head, a halo invisible to all, but visible to me, and in which were blended, in a strange amalgam, the rays of Art and the glory of the Martyr. Fancioulle brought, by a certain special grace, something divine and supernatural into even the most extravagant buffooneries. My pen trembles, and the tears of an ever-present emotion well up in my eyes as I try to describe to you that never-to-be-forgotten evening. Fancioulle proved to me, in a compelling, irrefutable way, that the intoxication of Art is more apt than anything else to veil the terrors of the abyss; such genius can perform a role at the edge of the tomb with a joy that prevents it from seeing the tomb,

A Heroic Death

lost, as it is, in a paradise that excludes any notion of death and destruction.

The entire audience, blasé and frivolous though it was, soon fell under the all-powerful spell of the performer's art. No one thought any more of death, mourning, or torment. Each abandoned himself serenely to the manifold delights afforded by the spectacle of a masterpiece of living art. Explosions of joy and admiration again and again shook the building's vaulted ceilings with the energy of continuous thunderclaps. Even the Prince, spellbound, added his own applause to that of his court.

However, to a discerning eye, his emotion was not untainted. Did he feel himself overcome by his despotic power? humiliated in his art of striking terror into the heart, and of numbing the spirit? frustrated in his hopes and humiliated in his plans? Such suppositions, not exactly justified, but not totally unjustifiable, passed through my mind as I studied the Prince's face, upon which a new pallor amplified the habitual pallor, like snow upon snow. His lips drew ever tighter, and his eyes were lit by an inner fire like that of jealousy and spite, even while he ostensibly applauded the talents of his old friend, the strange buffoon, who parodied death so well. At one point, I saw his Highness lean towards a little page who was seated behind him, and whisper something in his ear. The comely boy's mischievous countenance lit up with a smile, and he hastily left the Prince's box as if to perform an urgent mission.

Minutes later a shrill and prolonged whistling sound, at once both ear-splitting and heart-rending, interrupted

A Heroic Death

Fancioulle in one of his finest moments. And from the place whence this unexpected disapproval had sounded, a child darted into a passageway, stifling his laughter.

Fancioulle, shaken from his dream, first closed his eyes, opened them again amazingly wide, opened his mouth as if struggling for breath, staggered slightly forwards, then slightly backwards, and fell stone dead on the boards.

Had the whistling sound, swift as a sword, really frustrated the executioner? Had the Prince anticipated the lethal efficacy of his ruse? There is room for doubt. Did he regret the demise of his dear, inimitable Fancioulle? It would be kind and reasonable to think so.

The guilty noblemen had enjoyed a comic spectacle for the last time. That same night they were erased from life.

Since then, many actors, rightly appreciated in their various countries, have come to perform at the court of ***; but none have ever been able to match the amazing talents of Fancioulle, nor risen to comparable patronage.

XXVIII. The Counterfeit Coin

As we left the tobacconist's shop, my friend was carefully sorting his change; into the left pocket of his waistcoat he slipped some small gold coins; into the right one, some little silver coins; into the left pocket of his trousers, several large copper coins, and finally, into the right pocket, a silver two-franc piece to which he had paid special attention.

"A singular and meticulous division!" I thought to myself.

We came across a pauper who held out his cap to us with a trembling hand. I can think of nothing more disquieting than the silent eloquence of those imploring eyes which contain, for the sensitive man who knows how to read them, at once humility and reproach. In them he finds something akin to that depth of complex emotion present in the tearful eyes of a dog being flogged.

My friend's offering was far more substantial than mine, and I said to him: "You are right; next to the pleasure of being astonished, there is none greater than that of causing surprise." — "The coin was fake," he answered calmly, as if to justify his prodigality.

But into my miserable brain, always busy seeking noon at two o'clock (what a tiresome faculty nature granted me!), there suddenly came the idea that such behaviour on the part of my friend was only excusable out of a desire to create an event in the life of that poor devil, perhaps even to discover the various consequences, dire or otherwise, that a counterfeit coin can have in the hands of a mendicant. Could it help

The Counterfeit Coin

generate some real money? Could it land him in jail? An innkeeper or a baker, for example, might have him arrested as a forger, or for circulating fake coins. Equally, the counterfeit coin might perhaps be, for some poor little speculator, the seed of several days' wealth. And so my imagination followed its course, lending wings to the spirit of my friend and drawing all possible deductions from all imaginable hypotheses.

But the latter abruptly shattered my reverie by recalling my own words: "Yes, you are right: there is no sweeter pleasure than to surprise a man by giving him more than he expected."

I looked into the whites of his eyes, and I was shocked to see that they shone with unquestionable candour. I then saw clearly that he had wanted to perform both a charitable act and negotiate a deal; to save forty pence and win the heart of God; to get free admission to Paradise; in short, to obtain charitable status at no expense. I could almost have forgiven him the desire for criminal pleasure of which I had just now thought him capable! I might simply have found it peculiar that he thought it amusing to compromise the poor; but I shall never pardon the ineptitude of his calculation. It is never excusable to be mean, but there is some merit in acknowledging it; what is beyond redemption is to do wrong out of sheer stupidity.

XXIX. The Generous Gambler

Yesterday, in a crowded street, I was jostled by a mysterious Being whom I had always wanted to know, and whom I recognised at once, though I had never seen him before. He undoubtedly felt a desire similar to my own, for he gave me, as he passed by, a meaningful wink to which I hastened to respond. I stayed close behind him, and soon I was following him down to a superb underground apartment that shone with a luxury which even the finest dwellings of Paris could never match. It seemed strange to me that I could have walked past this prestigious retreat so often without ever noticing the doorway. Inside there reigned an exquisite, almost intoxicating atmosphere which made one forget instantly all the tedious horrors of life; here one inhaled a mystical serenity, similar to that which the lotus-eaters must have felt when, disembarking on an enchanted isle illuminated by the glow of an eternal afternoon, they felt arise within them, lulled by the melodious music of the cascades, the desire never to return home, never to see again their wives and their children, and never again to brave the ocean's swell.

Here were strange faces of men and women, marked by a fatal beauty which I felt I had seen before, but in times and places that I could not precisely recall, and which inspired in me a fraternal affinity rather than the fear that is usually aroused when one is confronted with the unknown. Were I to attempt to define in some way the singular expression on their faces, I should say that never had I seen eyes that shone more emphatically with the horror of ennui and the unending desire to feel alive.

By the time we were seated my host and I had become firm friends. As we dined, we imbibed vast quantities of many extraordinary wines, and what seemed to me no less extraordinary was that after several hours I was no more inebriated than he was. But gaming, that divine pleasure, had regularly interrupted our frequent libations, and I must confess that as we played, I gambled and lost my soul with heroic nonchalance and frivolity. The soul is such an intangible thing, so often unavailing and sometimes so inconvenient, that I experienced, regarding that loss, only slightly less emotion than if I had lost my visiting card whilst out walking.

For a long time we smoked cigars, of which the incomparable savour and aroma imparted to the soul a nostalgia for unknown lands and pleasures. Intoxicated with all these delights I seized an overflowing goblet, and in an outburst of familiarity which did not appear to displease him I cried: "To your immortal health, old Buck!"

We discussed the universe, its creation, and its future destruction. We spoke of the century's great concept, that of progress and perfectibility, and more generally of all forms of human conceit. On this subject, His Highness was a source of diverting and irrefutable pleasantries, expressing himself with an elegance of diction and an assuredness in his banter, the like of which I have never encountered, even among the most celebrated raconteurs of society. He explained to me the absurdity of the various philosophies that have hitherto taken possession of the human brain, even deigning to confide to me some fundamental principles, the benefits and ownership of which I am not minded to share with anyone. In no way did he bemoan the bad reputation that he universally enjoys, assuring me that he was as keen as anyone to do

The Generous Gambler

away with superstition and confessing that he had only once feared for his own power on the day he heard a preacher, more subtle than his peers, exclaim from the pulpit: "My dear brothers, never forget that when you hear men lauding the progress of science, the finest ruse of the Devil is to persuade you that he does not exist!"

The recollection of that famous orator led us naturally onto the subject of academies, and my strange friend stated that in many cases he did not disdain to inspire the pen, the word, and the conscience of pedagogues, and that he attended, albeit invisibly, most scholarly events.

Encouraged by so much generosity, I asked him for news of God, and whether he had seen him recently. He replied, with an insouciance tinged with sadness: "We greet one another when we meet, but as two old gentlemen, in whom an innate politeness cannot quite extinguish the memory of old grudges."

It is doubtful that His Highness had ever granted so long an audience to a mere mortal, and I had no wish to take advantage. When at last shivering dawn cast its light on the windows, this famous personage, sung by so many poets and served by so many philosophers who work unwittingly for his glory, said to me: "I want you to take away a pleasant memory of me and to show you that I, of whom so much ill is said, can sometimes be a *good* devil, to use of one of your vulgar expressions. To compensate for the irremediable loss of your soul, I shall give you the stake that you would have won had fate been on your side, namely the possibility of relieving and overcoming for the rest of your life the bizarre sickness of Ennui, the source of all your ills and your woeful lack

The Generous Gambler

of progress. Never will you forge a desire that I shall not help you to realise; you will reign over your lowly peers; you will enjoy flattery and even adoration; silver, gold, diamonds and exquisite palaces will seek you out and beg you to accept them, without your having to make any effort to attain them; you will be free to roam from country to country as often as your fancy ordains; you will savour an endless intoxication of delights, in magical lands where it is always warm and the women smell as sweet as the flowers, etcetera, etcetera…", he added as he rose and took his leave of me with a pleasant smile.

Had it not been for fear of humiliating myself before such a large assembly, I should gladly have prostrated myself at the feet of this generous player, to thank him for his extraordinary charity. But after I had left him, dire misgivings began to enter my breast; I no longer dared trust such prodigious good fortune, and as I retired to my bed that night, still idiotically saying my prayers through force of habit, I kept repeating in my semi-slumber: "O Lord my God, make sure the Devil keeps his word!"

XXX. The Rope

To Édouard Manet

"Illusions," said a friend of mine, "are perhaps as numerous as relationships between men, or between men and things. And when the illusion disappears, that is, when we see the person or the fact as they exist detached from ourselves, we experience a bizarre sentiment that is half regret for the vanished phantom, half agreeable surprise at the novelty of the real thing. If there is one phenomenon that is obvious, banal, always the same, and of a nature that is impossible to mistake, it is maternal love. It is as difficult to conceive of a mother without maternal love as of a light without heat; is it not therefore perfectly legitimate to attribute to maternal love all a mother's actions and words concerning her child? And yet, listen to this little story, where I was totally taken in by the most natural of illusions.

"As a professional painter, I am accustomed to study closely the faces and expressions of people whom I encounter, and you know what pleasure we derive from that faculty which renders life more vivid and meaningful to our eyes than to those of other men. In the rural district where I live, where large areas of green still separate the buildings, I often used to observe a child whose spirited and mischievous demeanour instantly won me over, more so than all the others. He posed for me more than once, and I would transform him either into a little gypsy, or an angel, or a mythological Cupid. I would make him carry a wanderer's fiddle, the crown of thorns and the nails of the Passion, and the torch of Eros. I was so taken by the child's tomfoolery that I finally asked his parents, who were poor people, to place him in my care, promising to dress him well, give him some

The Rope

pocket money and ask nothing more of him than to clean my brushes and run my errands. The child, once spruced up, became a delight, and the life he led with me seemed like paradise to him, compared to the one he had suffered in the parental hovel. It must however be said that the little fellow's odd spells of precocious melancholy disturbed me at times, and he also developed an immoderate taste for sweetmeats and liqueurs; so much so that one day, when I noticed that despite my many warnings he had been pilfering yet again, I threatened to send him back to his parents. I then had to go out, and business matters kept me away for quite some time.

"Imagine my horror and bewilderment when, on returning home, the first thing that met my eyes was my little fellow, the mischievous little companion of my life, hanging from the wooden panel of a cupboard! His feet almost touched the floor; a chair, which he had no doubt kicked away, lay upended beside him; his head was twisted convulsively to one side; his face was swollen, and his wide open, chillingly staring eyes gave an initial impression of life. Taking him down was not as easy a task as you might think. He was already very stiff, and I felt an inexplicable reluctance to let him fall heavily to the floor. I had to support his entire weight with one arm and use my free hand to cut the rope. But I was not yet done; the little devil had used a very thin cord that had dug deep into his flesh, so I had to gently prise it out with fine scissors from between two folds of swollen flesh in order to free his neck.

"I omitted to mention that I had called out for help, but my neighbours all refused to come to my aid, thereby remaining true to the customs of civilized men, who for

The Rope

some reason will have nothing to do with a suicide. Eventually a doctor arrived and declared that the child had been dead for several hours. Later, when we had to undress him for burial, the body was so stiff we were unable to bend the limbs, so we were obliged to cut away the garments in order to remove them.

"The police officer, to whom of course I had to report the incident, eyed me sceptically and said: 'This looks suspicious!', motivated no doubt by an ingrained bias and a professional need to intimidate, on the off-chance, both innocent and guilty alike.

"There remained one final task to perform, the mere thought of which filled me with dread: the parents had to be informed. My feet refused to take me there. I finally plucked up the courage, but to my great astonishment, the mother remained unmoved. Not a single tear escaped from the corner of her eye. I put this strange anomaly down to the extreme horror she must be feeling, and I recalled the well-known saying: 'The most terrible grief is silent grief.' As for the father, all he could find to say in a half obtuse, half pensive way was: "It's perhaps for the best after all; he would have come to a bad end anyway!"

"Meanwhile the body was laid out on my sofa, and with the help of a servant I was taking care of the final details when the mother entered my studio. She said she wished to see her son's body. To be fair I could not prevent her from indulging her grief by refusing her that last sombre consolation. Then she asked me to show her the place where her child had hanged himself. 'Oh no, madame' I replied, 'that would be too upsetting for you.' But as my eyes turned involuntarily towards the fatal

The Rope

wardrobe I realised, with a mixture of disgust, horror, and anger, that the nail was still fixed to the panel with a long piece of rope still dangling from it. I quickly leapt forward to remove those last vestiges of the tragic misadventure, and as I was about to hurl them out through the open window, the poor woman grasped my arm and said in an irresistible voice: 'Oh please sir, let me have that! Please, I beg you.' I imagined that her despair had so distressed her that she was now overcome with tenderness for what had served as the instrument of her son's death, and she wished to keep it as a gruesome but cherished memento. And she took possession of the nail and the rope.

"At last the whole affair was over! All I had to do now was get back to work even more assiduously than usual to gradually expunge the memory of that little corpse with its wide-eyed stare that still haunted the recesses of my brain. But the next day I received a bundle of letters, some from tenants in the house, others from neighbouring houses; one from the first floor, another from the second, another from the third, and so on; some in a semi-humorous style, as though seeking to disguise beneath an apparent jocularity the eagerness of their request; others were brazenly shameless and poorly spelt; but all had the same purpose, namely, to obtain from me a piece of the sinister and beatific rope. Among the signatories there were, I have to say, more women than men; but believe me when I say that they were by no means all from the lower classes. I have kept those letters.

"And then it suddenly dawned on me why the mother had been so keen to snatch the rope from me, and by what commerce she intended to be consoled."

XXXI. Vocations

In a beautiful garden, where the rays of an autumnal sun seemed to linger at their pleasure, under a sky already tinged with green, where golden clouds drifted by like floating continents, four spruce young lads were deep in conversation, having no doubt grown weary of their games.

One said: "Yesterday I was taken to the theatre. In great, sombre palaces set against a backdrop of sea and sky, men and women who are serious and sad, but much more beautiful and elegant than everyday people, speak in lilting tones. They threaten one another, plead disconsolately with one another, and sometimes they place their hand on a dagger that is thrust inside their belt. Ah! It is a wonderful sight! The women are far more beautiful and a lot taller than the ones who come to our house, and although their big hollow eyes and fiery cheeks give them a fearsome look, you cannot help but like them. You are afraid and you feel like crying, but at the same time you are happy. And strange as it may seem it makes you want to dress like them, say and do the same things, and speak like they do...."

One of the four children, who was no longer listening to his playmate's monologue and was gazing intently at the sky, suddenly said: "Look, look up there! Do you see *him*? He is sitting on that lonely little flame-red cloud that is moving slowly across the sky. *He* seems to be watching us too."

"Who exactly?" asked the others.

"God!" he answered, with the utmost conviction. "Ah, but he's already moving further away; soon you won't be

Vocations

able be able to see him anymore. He must be visiting all the countries of the world. Look, he's about to disappear behind those trees on the horizon...and now he's going down behind the church tower…Ah! now we can't see him anymore!" He maintained his gaze for a long time, staring at the line that separates heaven and earth, his eyes aglow with an ineffable expression of ecstasy and regret.

"He's so dumb, that one, with his God that only he can see!" said the third boy, whose whole being exuded exceptional vivacity and vitality. "I'm going to tell you about something that happened to me that has never happened to you, something a lot more interesting than your theatres and your clouds. My parents recently took me on an outing, and as the inn where we stopped for the night did not have enough beds for all of us, it was decided that I should sleep in the same bed as my nanny." He drew his comrades closer and spoke in a quieter voice. "It's an odd feeling, you know, being in bed with your nanny in the dark. As I lay awake, I thought it might be fun to stroke her arms and neck and shoulders as she slept. She is a lot more buxom than most other women, and her skin was so soft it felt like silk. It gave me such pleasure that I would have carried on for longer had I not been afraid she might wake up and what might happen if she did. I buried my face in the mane of hair that lay across her back, and it smelled just as good, believe me, as the flowers in this garden do today. Try it if you get the chance, and you'll see what I mean!"

The young author of this stupendous revelation told his story with eyes wide open in a sort of trance at what he still felt, and the rays of the setting sun playing across

Vocations

the russet curls of his unkempt hair seemed to ignite a demonic aureole of passion. It was easy to tell that this one would not waste his life seeking the Divinity in the clouds, and that he would frequently find it elsewhere.

Finally, the fourth boy said: "You know that I seldom have much fun at home. No one ever takes me to a play, my tutor is too stingy; God does not care if I am bored, and I don't have a pretty nanny to pamper me. I have often thought that I might like to travel, roaming wherever chance takes me, discovering new places with no one to worry about me. I am never happy wherever I am, and I always think that I would be better off somewhere else. Anyway, at the last village fair I saw three men who were living the sort of life I would like to live. You three did not even notice them. They were tall, swarthy, and proud despite their ragged clothes, and their manner suggested that were perfectly self-sufficient. Their huge, dark eyes lit up while they made music, a music so striking that it made you want to either dance or cry, or do both at the same time, and you felt as though you would go mad if you listened for too long. One of them, drawing his bow across his violin, seemed to be telling a tale of heartbreak; the second one, his little hammer skipping over the keys of a small piano hanging from a strap around his neck, appeared to be mocking his neighbour's sorrow, while the third would clash his cymbals every now and then with extraordinary force. They were so pleased with themselves that they carried on playing their wild music even after the crowd had dispersed. Finally, they picked up their takings, hoisted all their belongings onto their backs, and decamped. I was curious to know where they lived, so I followed them at a distance to the edge of a forest, and that is when I

Vocations

realised that they actually didn't live anywhere.

"One of them said: 'Should we pitch the tent?'

"'I'd rather not!' replied his friend. 'It's such a lovely night!'

"The third one said, as he counted the takings: 'Those people have no feel for music, and their wives dance like she-bears. Fortunately, in a month's time we'll be in Austria, where people are more congenial.'

"Perhaps we would be better off heading for Spain; the season's nearly over, so let's get going before the rain arrives, and only get our whistles wet,' said one of the other two.

"You see, I've remembered every detail. They each drank a cup of brandy and then they went to sleep, looking up at the stars. At first I wanted to beg them to take me along with them and to teach me to play their instruments; but I didn't dare, partly because I always have trouble deciding about anything, and partly because I was afraid I'd be caught before I was clear of France."

Judging by the indifferent air of his three friends I concluded that this little fellow belonged to the circle of the misunderstood. I studied him closely; there was something precociously intense about the look in his eyes that generally alienates sympathy, but which for some reason so aroused mine that I briefly had the bizarre notion I might have a brother I had never known.

The sun had gone down. Solemn night had taken its

Vocations

place. The boys went their separate ways, each to fulfil his own destiny as chance and circumstance would decide, to bring scandal upon his family and to gravitate towards glory or dishonour.

XXXII. The Thyrsus

To Franz Liszt

What is a thyrsus? In its religious and poetic sense, it is a sacerdotal emblem in the hands of a priest or priestess when celebrating the divinity whose interpreters and servants they are. But physically it is just a stick, a simple stick, a hop-pole, a vine prop, dry, hard, and straight. Meandering capriciously around it, stems and flowers frolic and play, some sinuous and elusive, others hanging like bells or upturned cups. And an amazing splendour flows forth from this delicate and striking complexity of lines and colours. Could it not be that the curved line and the spiral are paying homage to the straight line, and twine about it in silent adoration? Could it not be that all those delicate petals and cups, those bursts of scents and colours, are performing a mystical fandango around the sacerdotal staff? And what foolhardy mortal will dare to decide whether the flowers and the vines were created for the pole, or whether the pole is just a means of showing off the beauty of the vines and the flowers? The thyrsus is the symbol of your astonishing duality, most powerful and venerated master, esteemed bacchanal of mysterious and impassioned Beauty. Never did a nymph, provoked by the indomitable Bacchus, shake her thyrsus over the heads of her distraught companions with as much energy and caprice as when you exercise your genius upon the hearts of your brothers. —The pole is your will: erect, firm, unshakeable; the flowers are the wanderings of your fancy around your will, the feminine element encircling the male with its prestigious pirouettes. Straight lines and arabesques—intention and expression, rigidity of the will and suppleness of the word, unity of aim and variety of method, the omnipotent and indivisible fusion of genius — what

The Thyrsus

analyst will have the outrageous temerity to divide and separate you?

Dear Liszt, through the mists, beyond the rivers, above the towns where pianofortes sing of your glory, where the printing-press translates your wisdom, wherever you may be, in the splendour of the eternal city or in the mists of dreamlike lands consoled by the nectar of Cambrinus, improvising songs of delectation or ineffable pain, or committing to paper your esoteric meditations, bard of eternal Pleasure and Pain, poet, philosopher, and artist, I salute you in immortality!

XXXIII. Get Drunk

You should always be drunk. It is all that matters. So as not to feel the terrible burden of Time on your shoulders, crushing you and weighing you down, you should always be drunk.

But on what? On wine, poetry, virtue, or whatever takes your fancy. But get drunk.

And if on the steps of a palace, the green grass of a ditch, or in the dreary solitude of your room, you should wake a little tipsy or even stone cold sober, ask the wind, the wave, the star, the bird, the clock, anything that moves, moans, rolls, sings or speaks, ask what time it is; and the wind, the wave, the star, the bird, the clock will reply: "It is time to get drunk! If you are not to be the martyred slave of Time, just get drunk and stay drunk! 0n wine, on poetry or on virtue, the choice is yours."

XXXIV. Already!

A hundred times already the sun had leapt, radiant or mournful, from the immense bowl of the sea whose edges are barely visible; a hundred times it had gone down, brilliant or morose, into its great evening bath. For several days we could study the far side of the firmament and decipher the celestial alphabet of the antipodes. And all the passengers sighed and groaned. It was as if the proximity of land enhanced their suffering. "When," they said, "will we stop being shaken in our sleep by the swell, and disturbed by a wind that snores louder than we do? When will we be able to eat meat that is not as salty as the hideous element that carries us? When will we be able to digest our meal in a chair that stays still?"

There were those who were thinking of home, who were missing their sullen, faithless wives and their noisy offspring. They were so distraught at the thought of their absent homeland that I think they would have eaten grass with greater relish than the beasts of the field.

At last the coast was sighted, and we saw, as we approached, that it was a magnificent and dazzling land. It seemed that the music of life flowed from it in a vague murmur; and that from its shores, rich with all kinds of greenery, there emanated, for miles around, a delicious odour of flowers and fruits.

Suddenly everyone was filled with joy; bad moods were banished, quarrels were forgotten, wrongs were mutually forgiven, planned duels were erased from memory, and acrimony vanished like smoke.

I alone was sad, inconceivably sad. Like a priest robbed of his divinity, I could not, without heart-rending

Already!

bitterness, take my leave of that monstrously seductive ocean, so infinitely varied in its terrifying simplicity, and which seems to embody and represent through its games, attractions, rages and smiles, the agonies and the ecstasies of all the souls that have lived, are living and who are yet to live!

As I bade farewell to that incomparable beauty I felt mortally despondent; and that is why when each of my companions said: "At last!", all I could utter was: "Already!"

And yet here was land. Land with all its sounds, passions, merchandise, and festivities; a magnificent, abundant land replete with promises, emanating an esoteric perfume of rose and musk, and the amorous murmur of the music of life.

XXXV. Windows

An open window can never reveal as much as a closed one. There is nothing more profound, more mysterious, more fertile, more ambiguous, or more revealing than a window lit by a single candle. What we see in daylight is always less interesting than what goes on behind a pane of glass. In that darkly lit space life lives, life dreams, life suffers.

Across undulating rooftops, I catch sight of a woman of mature years, already wizened, poverty-stricken, permanently stooped, housebound. From her face, her attire, her demeanour, from almost nothing, I have recreated that woman's story, or rather her legend, and sometimes I tell it to myself with tears in my eyes.

Had it been a poor old man, I could have made up his story just as easily.

And I go to bed, proud of having lived and suffered with someone other than myself.

Perhaps you will ask if I have divined the true story. Does the reality that exists outside my own thoughts really matter, so long as the story helps me to live, to feel that I am, and what I am?

XXXVI. The Desire to Paint

Unhappy perhaps the man, but happy the artist who is torn by desire.

I long to paint a woman whom I have rarely seen, who vanished so soon, like a thing of beauty the traveller must regretfully leave behind in the night. How long it is since I last saw her!

She is not merely beautiful, she is astonishing. She exudes an abundance of darkness: all that she inspires is nocturnal and profound. Her eyes are two caverns that glisten with arcane mystery: her gaze illuminates like a lightning flash, an explosion in the dark.

I could compare her to a black sun if one could conceive of a sun that is black yet diffuses light and happiness. But she is more readily suggestive of the moon, which has undoubtedly touched her with its formidable influence; not the pale moon of idylls that resembles a frigid bride, but the sinister and intoxicating moon suspended in the depths of a stormy night, jostled by the scudding clouds; not the discreet and peaceful moon that visits pure men as they sleep, but a moon torn from the sky, conquered and rebellious, that the witches of Thessaly harshly constrain to dance upon the terrified grass.

Behind her delicate brow reside a tenacious will and a lust for prey. Yet in the rest of that disquieting countenance, where inquisitive nostrils inhale the unknown and the impossible, laughter of ineffable grace bursts forth from the generous red lips and white teeth of an exquisite mouth, conjuring the miracle of a superb flower burgeoning in a volcanic soil.

The Desire to Paint

There are women who stir a desire to win and enjoy them; but this one imparts a yearning to slowly expire beneath her gaze.

XXXVII. Favours of the Moon

The Moon, who is caprice itself, looked in through your window as you lay sleeping in your cradle, and said to herself: "I really like this child."

And softly descending her stairway of clouds, she passed silently through the windowpane. Then she lay upon you with a mother's supple tenderness and left her colours on your face. That is why your eyes are green and your cheeks are so extraordinarily pale. It was when you gazed upon this visitor that your eyes grew so strangely wide, and she held you so close and so tenderly that the memory of it still moves you to tears.

However, in the expansion of her joy, the Moon pervaded the room with phosphorescence, like a luminous poison; and that living radiance thought and said: "You must forever endure the influence of my caress. You will be beautiful as I am beautiful. You will love what I love and what loves me: water, clouds, silence, night; the vast green sea; formless and multiform water; the place where you will never be; the lover you will never know; gigantic flowers; intoxicating perfumes; cats that lie languidly on pianos, moaning like women in soft, husky voices!

"And you will be loved by my lovers and courted by my courtiers. You will be the queen of green-eyed men, who too have felt my nocturnal caress; queen of those that love the sea, the vast tumultuous green sea, the formless and multiform water, the place where they are not, the women they do not know, the sinister flowers that resemble censers of an unknown religion, the odours that trouble the will, and the voluptuous wild beasts that are the emblems of their madness."

Favours of the Moon

And that is why, my sweet, pampered, star-crossed child, I am now lying at your feet, seeking in your whole person the image of the fearsome goddess, the fateful godmother, the poisonous wet-nurse of all who fall under her spell.

XXXVIII. Which Is the Real One?

I once knew a certain Benedicta, who imbued all around her with a sense of the ideal, and from whose eyes flowed the desire for greatness, beauty, glory, and all that makes us believe in immortality.

But that miraculous girl was too beautiful to live for long, and she died just a few days after I met her. I buried her myself, on a day when the incense of spring wafted over the graveyard. I buried her with my own hands, sealed inside a coffin of wood, perfumed and incorruptible like an Indian casket.

And as my eyes remained fixed upon the spot where I had buried my treasure, I suddenly saw a small figure, who bore a remarkable resemblance to the deceased, stomping over the freshly turned soil in a bizarre, hysterical frenzy. "Look at me!" she said in a fit of laughter: "I am the real Benedicta, a notorious libertine! And to punish you for your blindness and folly you shall love me just as I am!"

But I was furious and replied: "No! no! no!" And to add more emphasis to my refusal I stamped so hard on the ground that my leg sank knee-deep into the newly dug grave, and now, like a wolf caught in a trap, I shall remain fastened, perhaps for ever, to the grave of the ideal.

XXXIX. A Thoroughbred

She is just plain ugly, and yet she is delightful!

Time and Love have marked her with their claws and have cruelly taught her how every minute and every kiss steal something of youth and freshness.

She is indeed ugly; she is, if you will, ant, spider, skeleton even; but she is also potion, magisterium, witchcraft; in short, she is exquisite!

Time has not defiled the sparkling harmony of her demeanour, nor the indestructible elegance of her armature. Love has not impaired the sensuality of her childlike breath; Time has ravaged nothing of her abundant mane, whose primitive odours exude all the devilish vitality of the Midi: Nîmes, Aix, Arles, Avignon, Narbonne, Toulouse, amorous and enchanting cities, blessed by the sun!

The sharp teeth of Time and Love have gnawed at her in vain; they have diminished none of the vague, eternal charm of her gamine breast.

Worn perhaps, but not wearied, and always heroic, she reminds you of one of those thoroughbred horses which the true connoisseur will always recognise, even when harnessed to a hackney carriage or a heavy cart.

And then she is so gentle and so fervent! She loves in an autumnal way; you might say that the coming of winter ignites a new flame in her heart, and the servility of her affection is never wearisome.

XL. The Mirror

A hideous man enters and looks at himself in the mirror.

"Why do you look at yourself in the mirror, since you can only view yourself with disgust?"

The hideous man replies: "Sir, in accordance with the immortal principles of '89, all men have equal rights; therefore I have the right to behold my reflection with pleasure or disgust; it concerns only me and my conscience."

In common sense terms I've no doubt that I was right; but from a legal standpoint he was not wrong.

XLI. The Harbour

A harbour is a delightful haven for a soul weary of life's tribulations. The vastness of the sky, the mobile architecture of the clouds, the changing colours of the sea, the flashing of the lighthouse, are a prism marvellously designed to enchant the eyes without ever tiring them. The slender vessels with their intricate rigging, swaying harmoniously with the swell, enhance the soul's perception of rhythm and beauty. And above all, there is a kind of mysterious, aristocratic pleasure for the man devoid of curiosity or ambition, in contemplating, from the comfort of a belvedere or the balustrade of a jetty, the hustle and bustle of people departing or returning, those who still have the strength of will that gives them the desire to travel and to enrich themselves.

XLII. Portraits of Mistresses

In a men's boudoir, namely a smoking room adjoining an upmarket gambling den, four men were smoking and drinking. They were neither young nor old, neither handsome nor ugly; but whether old or young, they all bore the distinctive mark of those veterans of debauchery, that elusive something, that cold, contemptuous dolefulness that so clearly says: "We have lived life to the full, and we are looking for something to love and to value."

One of them brought up the subject of women. It would have been wiser not to have mentioned the subject, but there exist intelligent men who are not averse to mundane conversation after they have had a few drinks. On such occasions one listens to the speaker in the same way one might listen to dance music.

"Every man," he said, "was once the age of a Cherub: that is the age when, if there are no nymphs about, one is quite happy to hug a tree. It is the first degree of love. The second degree is when one begins to choose. The ability to deliberate marks the onset of decadence. That is when the real search for beauty begins. For my part, gentlemen, I am proud to say that I have long since arrived at the definitive third stage, when beauty itself is no longer enough, unless it is seasoned with perfume, jewellery, and the like. I would even confess that I sometimes aspire to an undiscovered bliss, to a kind of fourth degree that is characterised by absolute calm. But throughout my life, except at the cherubic age, I have been more susceptible than other men to the enervating stupidity and the irritating mediocrity of women. What I most admire in animals is their candour. Consider then what I had to suffer at the hands of my last mistress.

Portraits of Mistresses

"She was the illegitimate daughter of a prince. Beautiful, that goes without saying; otherwise, why would I have taken her? But she ruined that great quality by an unseemly, twisted ambition. She was a woman who always wanted to play the man. 'You're not a man!' 'Ah! if only I were a man!' 'Of the two of us, it is I who am the man!' Such were the intolerable refrains that emerged from a mouth from which I simply wanted songs to issue forth. If I expressed admiration for a book, a poem, or an opera, she would immediately retort: 'You think that you speak with authority? what would you know about authority?' and she would pick an argument.

"One fine day she took up chemistry; so from then on there was always a glass mask between her lips and mine. Added to that she was extremely prudish. If on occasion I made an amorous gesture, she would recoil like a sensitive plant."

"How did it end?" asked one of the others. "I never knew you were so patient."

"God," he replied, "supplied the cure along with the disease. One day I found that Minerva seeking ideal authority in the arms of my valet, in a situation which caused me to retire discreetly to spare their blushes. That evening I paid them their arrears and dismissed them both."

"As far as I'm concerned," continued the interrupter, "I have only myself to blame. Happiness came knocking and I failed to recognise it. Fate recently granted me the enjoyment of a woman who was indeed the sweetest, most submissive, and most devoted of creatures, always ready, but devoid of enthusiasm. 'Of course I will, since that is what you want,' was her standard response. Were you to give a sound thrashing to that wall or this sofa you would elicit more sighs from them than my most ardent amorous advances ever drew from my mistress's breast. After a year of cohabitation she confessed to me that she had never experienced pleasure. I grew weary of this one-sided duel, so that incomparable girl married someone else. When years later I felt the urge to look her up, she showed me her six beautiful children, and said: 'Well, my dear friend, the wife is still as chaste as your mistress was.' Nothing had changed. I miss her every now and then; I should have married her."

The others started to laugh, and the third took his turn to speak:

"Gentlemen, I have known delights that you have perhaps overlooked. I speak of the comic aspect of love, which however does not preclude admiration. I admired my last mistress more, I suspect, than you loved or hated yours. And everyone admired her as much as I did. Whenever we went to a restaurant, the other diners would stop eating to look at her. Even the waiters and barmaid felt a contagious elation and neglected their duties. In short, I shared my life for some time with this living phenomenon. She could chew, crunch, devour and swallow in the most dainty and casual way imaginable. For a long time I was enchanted by her. She had such a sweetly wistful, English, romantic way of saying: 'I'm hungry'. And she repeated these words day and night, revealing the prettiest teeth in the world, which I found both touching and comical. I could have made a fortune exhibiting her at fairs as a polyphagous monster. I fed

Portraits of Mistresses

her well, but she left me all the same."

"For a purveyor of victuals, no doubt?"

"Something like that; some clerk in the supply corps who managed to pull a few strings to provide the poor child with the rations of several soldiers. At least, so I imagine."

The fourth man took his turn to speak. "I've suffered dreadfully", he said, "from the opposite of what selfish women are usually accused of. I find it quite unseemly that over-privileged people like you are complaining about your mistresses' imperfections!"

This was said in a most serious tone, by a man of gentle and sedate appearance, possessed of an almost clerical countenance that was incongruously lit by clear grey eyes that seemed to say: "I expect!" or "You must!" or even "I never forgive!"

"If you, G**, nervous as I know you to be, or you two, K** and J**, cowardly and superficial as you are, if any of you had been paired with a certain woman I knew, you would have either made good your escape, or died. I, as you see, managed to survive. Imagine someone incapable of error, whether it involves sentiment or judgment; imagine a disconcerting serenity of mind, a devotion devoid of airs and graces; kindness without weakness, firmness without harshness. My love story is like an endless voyage on a surface as pure and polished as a mirror, dizzyingly monotonous, reflecting all my feelings and actions with the ironic precision of my conscience, so that I could not permit myself an unreasonable action or emotion without becoming immediately aware of my conjoined spectre's silent reproach. Love seemed more like a tutelage. How many stupid things she stopped me from doing, which I regret not having done! How many debts I settled in spite of myself! She deprived me of all the benefits I might have derived from my own folly. With a cold, impervious regime, she blocked all my whims. Worst of all, she expected no gratitude once the danger had passed. I have lost count of the times I stopped myself from grasping her by the throat and shouting: 'Show me your imperfections, you wretch, so that I can love you without malaise and vexation!' For several years I admired her with a heart filled with hatred. In the end, I was not the one who died!

"Ah!" said the others, "then she is dead?"

"Yes. It could not continue like that. For me love had become an overwhelming nightmare. Conquer or die, as they say in politics, such the choice that destiny decreed. One evening, beside a lake, after a depressing woodland walk, her eyes reflecting the serenity of heaven, and my heart gripped by thoughts of hell…

"What!"

"What's that?"

"What do you mean?"

"It was inevitable. I have too great a sense of justice to strike, humiliate, or dismiss an irreproachable servant. But I had to reconcile that sentiment with the horror she inspired in me; rid myself of her without disrespecting her. What else could I have done with her, since she was perfect?"

The other three looked at him with a sort of vague bewilderment, as though feigning incomprehension, or tacitly avowing themselves incapable of taking such extreme action, despite the ample justification.

Then they ordered fresh bottles, to kill Time that has such a robust lifespan, and to accelerate Life that drifts along so slowly.

XLIII. The Gallant Marksman

As the carriage made its way through a wood, he had it stop at a shooting gallery, saying that he would like to fire off a few rounds to kill Time. Is not the slaying of that monster a man's most natural and legitimate occupation? — And he gallantly offered his hand to his dear, adorable, execrable wife, that mysterious woman to whom he owes so much pleasure, so much pain, and perhaps a fair share of his genius.

Several bullets went wide of the intended target; one even became lodged in the ceiling, and as the charming creature laughed hysterically, mocking her husband's ineptitude, he promptly turned to her and said: "You see that doll over there, the snooty-looking one on the right with its nose in the air? Well, my angel, I'm going to imagine it's you!" He closed both eyes and pulled the trigger. The doll was neatly decapitated.

Then, bowing to his dear, adorable, execrable wife, his inexorable, implacable Muse, and respectfully kissing her hand, he added: "Ah, my dear angel, I thank you most humbly for my expertise!"

XLIV. Soup and the Clouds

My -darling little minx was serving me dinner, and through the open dining-room window I gazed at the moving architecture that God creates from vapour, the marvellous constructions of the ethereal, and I thought to myself: "These phantasmagoria are almost as exquisite as the eyes of my beautiful darling, the monstrous little green-eyed minx."

Suddenly, I received a violent punch in the back, and I heard a seductive, husky, hysterical voice, a voice rendered hoarse by too much *eau-de-vie*, the voice of my sweet little darling, saying: "Are you ever going to eat your soup, you s*** b*** of a cloud merchant?"

XLV. The Shooting-range and the Cemetery

Cemetery View Inn. —"An odd name for an inn," thought our traveller; "but guaranteed to raise a thirst! This innkeeper must certainly appreciate Horace and the disciples of Epicurus. Perhaps he is even familiar with the profound philosophy of the ancient Egyptians for whom no feast was complete without a skeleton, or some other reminder of life's brevity."

He went in, drank a glass of beer as he sat facing the tombstones, slowly smoking a cigar. Then the idea occurred to him to go down to the cemetery, where the grass was so tall and inviting and the sun shone so brightly.

Indeed, the light and the heat were mightily intense; it was as if the intoxicated sun lay sprawled across a magnificent carpet of flowers that were fertilised by decomposition. The air was buzzing with the sounds of life—the life of minuscule creatures—punctuated at regular intervals by the crackling of gunfire from a nearby shooting-range, that sounded like champagne corks exploding to the background of a muted symphony.

Then, with the sun searing his brain and surrounded by the pervading perfume of Death, he heard a voice whispering from beneath the grave where he was sitting. And that voice said: "A curse on your targets and your rifles, you rowdy mortals, who care so little for the dead and their sacred rest! Damn your ambitions and your strategies, restless mortals who come to learn the art of killing next to the sanctuary of Death! If only you knew how easy it is to win the prize, to hit the target, and how all save Death is nothingness, you industrious mortals would not tire yourselves so, and you would disturb less frequently the slumber of those who have long since attained their Goal—the only true goal of a loathsome existence!"

XLVI. The Lost Halo

"Hey, what's this! You here, my friend? You, in a place of ill repute! You, the imbiber of apotheoses! you, the ambrosia eater! This really is a surprise!"

"My dear fellow, you know my dread of horses and carriages. Just now, as I hastily made my way across the boulevard, picking my way through the mud and the chaos of traffic, where death arrives at a gallop from every direction, my halo was suddenly knocked off my head onto the filthy tarmac. I didn't have the courage to pick it up. I considered it less disagreeable to lose my insignia than to suffer broken bones. And then, I told myself, it is an ill wind that blows nobody any good. I can now go about incognito, commit dastardly acts, and give myself over to debauchery like any ordinary mortal. And here I am, just like you, as you see!"

"You should at least put up a notice about your halo, or notify the police."

"Good Lord no! I like it here. You are the only one to have recognised me. Besides, I am tired of decorum, and the thought of some second-rate poet finding it and having the audacity to put it on his head just fills me with delight. Making someone happy is such a joy, especially if it is someone I can laugh at! What if it was X***, or Z***, eh? Wouldn't that be a hoot!"

XLVII. Mademoiselle Bistouri

As I approached the outer limits of the city with its dimly lit streets, I felt an arm slide gently under mine, and I heard a voice whisper in my ear: "Are you a doctor, monsieur?"

I turned to discover a tall, robust, wide-eyed young woman, slightly rouged, her hair and bonnet strings dancing in the breeze.

"No, I am not a doctor. Let me pass."

"Oh yes! you are a doctor. I know you are. Come home with me. You won't be sorry, I promise." "Of course I'll come and see you, but later, after you've seen a doctor, for heaven's sake!" – "Aha!" she said, still clinging to my arm and bursting into laughter. "You're a fun-loving doctor. I've known a few like you. Come on."

I really do love a mystery, because I always hope to unravel it. So I let myself be led by my companion, or rather by this unforeseen enigma.

I will not bother to describe the hovel; it can be found in works by a number of well-known old French poets; except that, a detail overlooked by Régnier, two or three portraits of renowned physicians hung on the walls.

How I was pampered! A blazing fire, mulled wine, cigars; and, as she proffered these delights while lighting a cigar for herself, the whimsical creature said: "Make yourself at home, my friend, make yourself comfortable. This will bring back memories of the hospital and the happy days of your youth.... Gosh! When did your hair go grey? It wasn't like that not so long ago, when you were a houseman with L***. I remember it was you that helped him with the major operations. How he loved to cut, trim and crop! You were the one that handed him the instruments, the thread and the swabs. And when the operation was over, he would look at his watch and proudly proclaim: 'Five minutes, gentlemen!' — You see, I get around a lot! I know these Gentlemen well!"

Moments later, switching to the more familiar *tu* and resuming her pet theme, she said: "You are a doctor, aren't you, sweetie?"

Her banal refrain so infuriated me that I sprang to my feet, shouting 'No, I am not!'

"A surgeon, then?"

"No! No! unless it would be to cut off your head, you s***d*** of a h***m***!"

"Wait," she went on, "I'll show you."

And she took from a cabinet a wad of papers, which turned out to be a collection of lithographic portraits by Maurin of eminent contemporary physicians, which had been displayed on the Quai Voltaire for several years already.

"Look! do you recognise this one?"

"Yes, it's X. His name is at the bottom, by the way; but I also happen to know him personally."

"I knew that too!... Look! that's Z, the one who used to

Mademoiselle Bistouri

say to his class when speaking of X: 'That monster who wears the blackness of his soul on his face', just because he disagreed with him on some subject or other! How we used to laugh about that in medical school at the time! Do you remember?... Look! there's K, who denounced to the authorities the insurgents he was treating at his hospital. That was during the riots. How is it possible that so handsome a man can have so little heart? ... This one is W, a renowned English physician; I managed to catch him when he came to Paris. He looks like a woman, doesn't he?"

As I picked up a little parcel tied with string, which had also been placed on the table, she said: "Wait a moment, those are the interns, and these ones here are the externs."

And she spread out in a fan formation several photographs of much younger faces.

"When we see each other again, you'll let me have your portrait, won't you, darling?"

"But," I said, in turn pursuing my own fixation, "what makes you think I'm a doctor?"

"It's because you're so kind and so good to women!"

"Peculiar logic," I said to myself.

"Oh! I am rarely mistaken; I have known quite a few of those gentlemen. I am so fond of them that I often visit them even if I am not ill, just to see them. Some just say coldly: 'You are not ill at all!' But there are others who understand me because I make eyes at them."

Mademoiselle Bistouri

"And when they don't understand you...?"

"Well, if I have bothered them for no reason, I leave ten francs on the mantelpiece.... Those people are so good and so kind! I came across a young intern at the *Pitié* hospital; he was so handsome, so refined, and he had to work so hard, poor boy! His friends told me he was penniless, because his parents were poor and unable to send him any money. That did it for me. After all, I am quite attractive, even if I'm not as young as I was. I said to him: 'Come and see me as often as you like. And don't be shy, I don't need the money.' But you will appreciate that I had to go about it in a roundabout sort of way; I didn't put it to him too bluntly, as I wouldn't want to humiliate the poor boy!... Anyway, would you believe it, I have an odd craving that I dare not mention to him... I'd love him to come and see me with his doctor's bag and his apron, maybe even with a little blood on it."

This was said in a very forthright manner, as a smitten suitor might declare to an actress he has fallen for: "I'd love to see you in the costume you wore in that famous role you created...."

I stubbornly persisted: "Do you remember when and how you first acquired this strange obsession?"

It was difficult getting through to her, but finally I succeeded. Then, wistfully and with downcast eyes, she replied: "I don't know..., I can't remember."

What oddities there are be found in a big city, if one knows how to roam and observe. Life is teeming with innocent monsters.

Mademoiselle Bistouri

My Lord God, you the Creator, you the Master, you who made Law and Liberty; you, the Sovereign that does not interfere; you, the Judge that pardons; you, the source of all motives and causes, who perhaps gave me a taste for horror in order to convert my soul, as healing is achieved with the scalpel; Lord, have pity, have pity on mad people, men and women alike! O Creator! can monsters exist in the eyes of Him who alone knows why they exist, how they were made, and how they might not have been made?

XLVIII. Anywhere Out of the World

Life is a hospital where each patient is consumed by a desire to change beds. One of them would rather suffer next to the stove, while another believes he would recover sooner by the window. I always have the feeling that I would be better off elsewhere, and the question of changing place is one that I am constantly discussing with my soul.

"Tell me, my soul, my poor frozen soul, what would you say to living in Lisbon? It must be very warm there, and you could bask in the sun like a lizard. It is a city by the sea, built of marble or so I've heard, and the inhabitants have such a loathing for vegetation that they've ripped up all the trees. That would be your kind of landscape, a landscape of light and mineral, with liquid to reflect them."

My soul makes no response.

"Since you like to combine repose with the moving spectacle, perhaps you would like to live in Holland, such a heavenly place. I am sure you would delight in a country whose image you have so often admired in museums. What about Rotterdam with its forests of masts, and ships moored outside the houses?"

My soul remains silent.

"Or perhaps Batavia would be more to your liking? That's where we'd find the spirit of Europe wedded to the beauty of the tropics."

Not a word. -- Might my soul be dead?

Anywhere Out of the World

"Are you now so indifferent that you find pleasure only in pain? If that is so, why not escape to lands that are analogies of Death? I'll get things organised for us, my poor troubled soul! We'll pack our bags and head for Tornio. We could go even further, to the outer limits of the Baltic; as far away from life as possible; we could set up home at the Pole, where the sun's slanting rays just skim the earth, and the slow alternations of light and dark exclude variety and increase monotony, that sister of oblivion. There we can bathe in a sea of darkness, and now and then, for our delight, the Aurora Borealis will send us its roseate garlands, like the reflections of an infernal firework display!"

At last my soul springs to life, and wisely exclaims: "Anywhere! Anywhere! Just so long as it is out of this world!"

XLIX. Let's Bash the Poor!

For two weeks I had remained confined to my room, surrounded by books that were all the rage at the time (sixteen or seventeen years ago); I refer to those books that profess to make people happy, wise, and wealthy, all in just twenty-four hours. I had thus digested, or rather swallowed, all the advice offered by those purveyors of public well-being who advise the poor to enslave themselves, or who persuade them that they are all kings without a throne. So it won't come as a surprise that I was in a state of mind bordering on vertigo or stupidity.

However, deep within my psyche I seemed to sense the obscure germ of an idea that is superior to the entire catalogue of dubious advice I had just perused. But it was just the idea of an idea, still infinitely vague.

And I left my room with an extreme thirst, because the inordinate appetite for bad literature engenders a proportionate requirement for the open air and some liquid refreshment.

I was about to enter a bar when a beggar held out his hat to me with one of those unforgettable glances that would topple thrones, if mind could move matter, or a hypnotist's eye could ripen grapes.

At the same time, I heard a voice whispering in my ear, a voice I knew well: it was that of a good Angel, or a good Demon, that follows me wherever I go. Since Socrates had his good Demon, why should I not I have my good Angel, and why should I not, like Socrates, have the honour of securing my own diploma of madness, signed by the subtle Lélut and the well-informed Baillarget?

Let's Bash the Poor!

There is a difference between Socrates's Demon and mine, in that his Demon only appeared to him to forbid, warn, prevent, whereas mine seeks to counsel, suggest, persuade. Poor Socrates only had a Demon of constraint; mine is a Demon of affirmation, a Demon of action and combat.

Now the voice whispered to me: "For a man to be equal to another he must prove it, and to be worthy of liberty he must earn it."

I immediately went for my beggar. A single punch caused his eye to close and swell up like a balloon. I broke one of my nails shattering two of his teeth, and as I did not feel I had the strength to lay the old fellow out cold right away, being of a sickly disposition and not much good at boxing, I grabbed him by the collar with one hand, by the throat with the other, and started bashing his head as hard as I could against a wall. I confess that I had taken the precaution of surveying the surrounding area to ensure that in such a quiet part of town I was unlikely to be disturbed by the police.

Then, after I had floored the enfeebled sexagenarian with a kick to his back strong enough to break his shoulder blades, I grabbed hold of a heavy branch that was lying on the ground and beat him with the determined energy of a cook trying to tenderise a steak.

Suddenly, —O miracle! O joy of the philosopher who proves the excellence of his theory! —I watched as that ancient carcass sat up, then sprang to its feet with an energy I could never have imagined in such a run-down machine, and, with hatred in his eyes that seemed to me

Let's Bash the Poor!

a good omen, the decrepit ruffian came at me, blackened both my eyes, broke four of my teeth, and with the same branch beat me to a pulp. My potent medication had restored his pride and given him back his life.

With various gestures I made him understand that I considered the matter closed; and getting back up on my feet with the satisfaction of a Porch sophist, I said to him: "Monsieur, you are my equal! Please do me the honour of sharing my purse; and remember, if you are truly philanthropic, that you must apply to all your brothers, when they ask you for alms, the same theory that it has pained me to test on you."

He swore to me that he understood my theory, and that he would heed my advice.

L. Good Dogs

To Mr Joseph Stevens

Never, even among the younger writers of my century, has my admiration for Buffon caused me to blush; but to-day it is not the soul of that painter of nature's splendour that I shall call to my aid. No.

I should prefer today to call upon Sterne, and say to him: "Descend from heaven, or rise from the Elysian Fields, to inspire in me, in praise of good dogs and poor dogs, a song worthy of such a sentimental, incomparable humourist as yourself. Come back astride that famous ass which always accompanies you in posterity's memory, and make sure that it is holding its immortal macaroon daintily between its lips."

Begone, academic muse! I will have no truck with that old prude. I call upon the familiar, town-dwelling, living muse to help me sing the praises of good dogs, poor dogs, grubby dogs, the ones everyone treats as rabid or flea-ridden, except that is for the poor, whose companions they are, and the poet, who looks upon them with a fraternal eye.

You can keep your foppish pedigree, your coxcomb quadruped, your Great Dane, King Charles, or pug, so pleased with themselves they dart between visitors' legs or jump up onto their laps, as if they are so sure of everyone's admiration, boisterous as children, dim as a floozy, and often as surly and insolent as a kitchen maid! Especially to be avoided are those shivering, idle four-legged serpents called whippets, that do not have enough smell in their pointed noses to pick up the scent of a friend, nor enough sense in their flat skulls to play dominoes!

Good Dogs

Back to your kennels, you tiresome parasites!

Back to your silk-lined, padded kennels! I celebrate the poor mud-caked dog, the homeless vagabond, the performing dog, the dog whose instinct, like that of the pauper, the gypsy, and the strolling player, is magically sharpened by necessity, that wonderful mother and true custodian of intelligence!

I extol the poor dogs that wander alone through the winding alleys of sprawling cities, those that have looked at some poor outcast and said with eyes that glow with sincerity: "Take me with you, and from our shared misery we might find some sort of happiness!"

"Where do dogs go?" Nestor Roqueplan once asked in an immortal article that he has doubtless forgotten about, and that only I and perhaps Sainte-Beuve still remember.

"Where do dogs go?" you ask, impercipient humans. They go about their business!

Business appointments, lovers' trysts. Through the fog, the snow, and the mud, in the scorching heat and the pouring rain, they roam far and wide, walking, running, squeezing under carriages, motivated by their fleas, their passions, their needs, and their obligations. Like us, they are up bright and early, to earn their living or pursue their pleasure.

There are those that sleep in derelict buildings and who come at the same time every day to beg for titbits at the kitchen door of the Palais-Royal; others arrive from miles around to share a meal, lovingly prepared for them

Good Dogs

by sexagenarian old maids, who devote their hearts to animals, since imbecilic man has no more use for them.

Others, crazed by concupiscence, escape from their parish like slaves in flight, and head into town to spend an hour or so cavorting with a comely bitch, somewhat negligent in her toilette, but proud and grateful for the attention.

And they all arrive on time, without so much as a diary, memo, or pocketbook.

Are you acquainted with dreary Belgium, and have you, like me, admired all those strapping dogs tethered to the handcarts of butchers, milkmaids and bakers, whose exuberant barking bears witness to the ostentatious pleasure they take in vying with their equine brothers?

And here are two that belong to a still more civilized order! Let me show you the room of an absent street performer: —a curtainless bed of painted wood, with crumpled flea-infested bedclothes, two straw chairs, a cast-iron stove, and a couple of battered musical instruments. What a dreary decor! But look at those two intelligent creatures, dressed in sumptuous yet tattered outfits, behatted like minstrels or soldiers, surveying with a sorcerer's vigilance the nameless concoction simmering on the lighted stove, in the middle of which stands a long wooden spoon, like one of those overhead masts that announce the completion of a building.

Is it not fitting that such dedicated troupers do not take to the road without having lined their stomachs with

Good Dogs

a good thick soup? Can you not forgive a little sensuality in those poor devils who day in day out have to face an indifferent public as well as the injustice of a director who pockets the lion's share of the takings and consumes more than the rations of four performers?

How many times have I watched with affection all those four-legged philosophers, willing, submissive, devoted slaves, that the republican dictionary might designate as *officials*, if the republic were not too preoccupied with the well-being of men to afford dogs some respect!

And how often have I thought that there must be a place (who really knows?), where so much courage, patience and hard work is rewarded, a special paradise for good dogs, for poor, grubby, despondent dogs. Doesn't Swedenborg affirm that there is one for the Turks and one for the Dutch?

The shepherds of Virgil and Theocritus expected, in payment for their songs, a good cheese, a flute from the best maker, or a she-goat with swollen udders. The poet who has lauded good dogs has received in recompense a fine waistcoat whose rich yet fading colour evokes autumn suns, the beauty of mature women, and late Indian summers.

No one who was present at the tavern in the Rue Villa-Hermosa will forget the good grace with which the painter removed his waistcoat in favour of the poet, so well did he understand that it is right and proper to extol the virtues of poor dogs.

Good Dogs

Likewise a magnificent Italian tyrant might once have offered the divine Aretino a gem-encrusted dagger or a courtly cloak in exchange for a precious sonnet or a curious satirical poem.

And whenever the poet dons the painter's waistcoat, he is reminded of the good dogs, the philosopher dogs, those late Indian summers, and the beauty of women in their prime.

Epilogue

With happy heart I went up to the citadel,
Whence I surveyed the town in all its amplitude,
Hospital, brothel, jail, abyss, perdition, hell,

Where bloom the evil flowers of human turpitude.
O Satan, you know well, as master of my pain,
That I did not go there to shed an idle tear,

But like an aging rake with his old chatelaine,
I wanted to grow drunk on that great concubine,
Whose infamous allurements make me young again.

And whether in the sheets of morning you recline
In heavy slumber still, or strut flamboyantly
In evening's braided veil, enlaced with golden twine,

I love you, capital of vice and infamy!
Your villains and your whores afford felicities
Unknown to any brute or vulgar philistine.

Counterpart Poems in Verse

(from *The Flowers of Evil*)

Her Tresses (A Hemisphere in Her Hair, page 48)

O tresses that enfold your shoulders with such grace!
O curls! O fragrance wafting nonchalantly there!
What rapture! And to fill the boudoir's sombre space
With memories that sleep in this luxuriant place,
I want to shake it like a kerchief in the air!

Asia, where languor dwells, Africa's scorching heat,
Those distant worlds, whose absent wonders are so rare,
Live in the depths of this ambrosial retreat!
While other spirits float on sounds of music sweet,
Mine, O my love! bathes in the perfume of your hair.

I'll go where trees and men live in serenity,
Beneath an ardent sun taking their languid ease.
Thick tresses, be the swell that lifts and carries me!
You hold, ebony sea, a dazzling reverie
Of masts and sails afloat upon a zephyr breeze:

A busy haven where my spirit can inhale
A flood of sound and colour, scent, and purity,
Where vessels glide on seas of amber, in full sail,
Unfolding wide their arms to greet the majesty
Of a pure sky where warmth resides eternally.

And I shall plunge my head in eager drunkenness
Into this black sea where the other is enclosed.
And my keen spirit, that the gentle waves caress,
Will know where you reside, O fecund idleness,
Eternal lullaby of sweet-scented repose!

Blue tresses, darkly flowing like a banner, where
I revel in the azure blue of skies afar.
Upon the downy fringes of your tangled hair
I ardently imbibe the mingled perfumes there,
The oil of coconut, the heady musk and tar.

Her Tresses

Always! forever! in your flowing locks entwined,
My hand will sow pearls, rubies, sapphires crystalline,
So that to my desire you never will be blind!
Are you not the oasis where I dream, the vine
Where I imbibe long draughts of your nostalgic wine?

Invitation to a Journey *(page 49)*

My sister, my heart,
How sweet to depart
To that faraway haven with you!
To languidly lie,
To love and to die
In a land that resembles you!
The damp suns that rise
In those nebulous skies
Seem to mirror the charm that appears
In the mystic disguise
Of your treacherous eyes,
Glistening through their tears.

There, all is order and beauty,
Luxury, calm, and ecstasy.

Furnishings fine,
Embellished by time,
Would decorate our room,
And flowers most rare
Their fragrance would share
With amber's heady perfume.
Mirrors ornate,
And walls with the weight
Of Orient's splendour hung,
All things there would speak
In the secret mystique
Of their gentle native tongue.

There, all is order and beauty,
Luxury, calm, and ecstasy.

Invitation to a Journey

See those vessels that brave
The wind and the wave
Rocking gently in their berth.
It is to inspire
Your every desire
That they come from the ends of the earth.
The sun goes down,
Setting the town,
The meadows and rivers alight
With jacinth and gold,
Our dreams unfold
In a gentle warming light.

There, all is order and beauty,
Luxury, calm, and ecstasy.

Evening Twilight (page 61)

Behold the charming evening, friend of villainy.
It comes like an accomplice, softly, stealthily.
The sky, like a great alcove, closes from the east,
And unforbearing man becomes a savage beast.

O cordial evening, so desired by those who say:
We have, without a doubt, done honest work today!
It is the evening that brings comfort and relief
To those whose spirit is beset by pain and grief,
The conscientious sage who rests his weary head,
Or the stooped labourer relieved to find his bed.

Meanwhile repulsive demons waken from their sleep,
Reluctantly, like those who have to earn their keep,
Colliding into blinds and shutters in their flight.
The wind springs up to fan the streetlamp's flickering light,
As Prostitution comes to life and spreads about,
A colony of ants letting its workers out,
In all directions carving out a secret track,
Like an invader planning a surprise attack.
It taints the city's heart with its clandestine plan,
Like a voracious worm that steals the food of Man.
We hear the sounds of sizzling kitchens here and there,
The clamour of theatres, orchestras ablare.
Cheap restaurants, where gamblers gather for their sport,
Begin to fill with harlots, swindlers and their sort,
And thieves, who never rest and know not charity,
Will soon begin their odious activity,
Stealthily forcing open strongboxes and doors
To eat for a few days and buy clothes for their whores.

Evening Twilight

In this dark hour, my soul, reflect on all this sin,
And close your ears to this cacophony of din.
This is the hour when sick men feel the greatest pain,
When dark Night grasps them by the throat, and they attain
Their final destined path toward the shared abyss.
Their sighs pervade the hospital. — No more the bliss
Of evenings spent at home, sharing a fragrant bowl
Of soup beside the fire, with a beloved soul.

But then, most of them are unable to recall
The comfort of the hearth and have not lived at all!

NOTES

Page 17: A *Confiteor* is a confession of sins and a plea for mercy in the Roman Catholic Mass.

Page 20: The woodland nymph *La Sylphide* appears in *Mémoires d'Outre-Tombe (Memoirs from Beyond the Grave)* by François-René de Chateaubriand (1768 – 1848), and in an eponymous ballet of 1832.

Page 27: *Rhadamanthys, Minos* and *Aeacus* were the judges of the dead, three demi-god ministers of Hades.

Page 34: 'King Log (*Le roi solveau*)' and 'the crane that will chew you up, swallow you down and kill you at his pleasure' are references to La Fontaine's fable *The Frogs Who Ask for a King*.

Page 37: Luc de Clapiers, marquis de *Vauvenargues* (1715–1747), was a French writer and moralist.

Page 64: *Santerre* was a French revolutionary who was appointed jailer of Louis XVI and reputedly ordered a drum-roll at the king's execution to drown out the sound of his voice.

Page 65: *Jean de La Bruyère* (1645 –1696) was a French philosopher and moralist, who was noted for his satire. *Blaise Pascal* (1623 –1662) was a French mathematician, physicist, inventor, philosopher, writer, and Catholic theologian.

Page 70: *Hebe* was the daughter of Zeus and the cupbearer for the gods and goddesses of Mount Olympus, serving their nectar and ambrosia until she married Heracles. Her successor was the divine hero *Ganymede*, a beautiful Trojan mortal with whom Zeus fell in love.

Page 93: *Cambrinus*, or *Gambrinus* is a legendary European culture hero celebrated as an icon of beer.

Page 98: *The witches of Thessaly* could refer to a book by the Latin poet Claudian (c. 370 – c. 404 AD). In his *First Book Against Rufinus*, Megaera, one of the Erinyes, in the guise of an old man, says to Rufinus: 'I have the gift of magic and the fire of prophecy is within

NOTES

me. I have learned the incantations wherewith Thessalian witches pull down the bright moon.'

Page 117: Mathurin *Régnier* (December 21, 1573 – October 22, 1613) was a French poet and satirist.

Page 118 Antoine Maurin (1793 - 1860) was a French lithographer.

Page 122: *Anywhere Out of the World*. The English title is borrowed from *The Bridge of Sighs,* a poem by Thomas Hood (1799 – 1845), whose work Baudelaire admired. *Batavia* was a port in the Dutch East Indies, now Jakarta, capital of Indonesia. *Tornio* is a port in Finland.

Page 124: Louis Francisque *Lélut* (1804–1877) was a French medical doctor and philosopher known for his works *Démon de Socrate* and *L'Amulette de Pascal*, where he stated that Socrates and Blaise Pascal were insane. Jules *Baillarger* (1809 –1890), was a French neurologist and psychiatrist.

Page 127: *Joseph Stevens (1816 –1892)* was a Belgian animal painter and engraver who befriended Baudelaire during his self-imposed exile in Brussels from 1864 to 1867.

Page 128: Louis-Victor-Nestor *Roqueplan* (1805 –1870) was a French journalist and theatre director. Charles Augustin *Sainte-Beuve* (1804 – 1869) was a prominent French literary critic.

Page 130: Emanuel *Swedenborg* (1688 –1772) was a Swedish theologian, scientist, philosopher, and mystic.

Page 131: Pietro *Aretino* (1492 –1556) was an influential Italian author, playwright, poet, and satirist.

Printed in Great Britain
by Amazon